T0193907

We Gon' Be Alright

A Message of Hope for Believers in a God of Social Justice

PETER J. SPANN

authorHOUSE®

AuthorHouse™
1663 Liberty Drive
Bloomington, IN 47403
www.authorhouse.com
Phone: 1 (800) 839-8640

Published by AuthorHouse 07/22/2019

ISBN: 978-1-7283-1231-6 (sc)
ISBN: 978-1-7283-1230-9 (e)

Library of Congress Control Number: 2019906132

Print information available on the last page.

This book is printed on acid-free paper.

Scripture quotations marked NLT are taken from the Holy Bible, New Living Translation, copyright © 1996, 2004, 2007. Used by permission of Tyndale House Publishers, Inc. Carol Stream, Illinois 60188. All rights reserved. Website

Scripture taken from The Holy Bible, King James Version. Public Domain

This book is for my wife Shurlonda and our 2 children Peter II and Anissa. As my family, you all inspire me to do the work that I am doing. Thank you for all of your continued support as I work to comfort the afflicted and hopefully from time to time afflict the comfortable.

"*Inspired by some of Hip-Hop's all-star truth-tellers, Peter Spann invites his readers to join a chorus of witnesses who will speak justice and practice hope. His unwavering confidence in God's will toward justice and human flourishing through sermonic proclamation gives me greater hope for African American churches and communities.*"

— *Kenyatta R. Gilbert, Professsor of Homiletics, Howard University School of Divinity.*

INTRODUCTION

"We were one people, indivisible in the sight of God, responsible to each other and for each other.

We, the black people, the most displaced, the poorest, the most maligned and scourged, we had the glorious task of reclaiming the soul and saving the honor of the country. We, the most hated, must take hate into our hands and by the miracle of love, turn loathing into love. We, the most feared and apprehensive, must take fear and by love, change it into hope. We, who die daily in large and small ways, must take the demon death and turn it into Life.

His head was thrown back and his words rolled out with the rumbling of thunder. We had to pray without ceasing and work without tiring. We had to know evil will not forever stay on the throne. That right, dashed to the ground, will rise, rise again and again."

— Maya Angelou (quoting Dr. Martin Luther King, Jr.) *I Know Why The Caged Bird Sings*

"We have troubles all around us, but we are not defeated. We do not know what to do, but we do not give up the hope of living. We are persecuted, but God does not leave us. We are hurt sometimes, but we are not destroyed. We carry the death of Jesus in our own bodies so that the life of Jesus can also be seen in our bodies."

– 2 Corinthians 4: 8-10

W e are living in a day and age where Christianity is under attack. I know that we hear that phrase so much that it is beginning to sound more like a cliché than a clarion call for the true followers of Christ to stand up. Normally when we hear that "Christianity is under attack," it is usually some conservative right-wing group using the cloak of Christianity to advance their causes that are usually more rooted in White conservative values rather than anything Jesus would have stood for.

However, those of us who truly study the scriptures and try to promote the beloved community and fulfill Christ's ministry to the least of these, we are usually described more as "civil or human rights activists" more than we are Christians. It's as if issues of justice, equality and a respect for the human dignity of all people are not considered as part of the core of Christianity, but more like a distant cousin or a subsection of the overall message of Jesus Christ. When those types of conclusions are made about those of us who clearly identify the work of Christ as embracing both salvation and social justice, I see it as fake news.

Fake news, simply put, is news distributed by major (as well as social media) news outlets that purposefully report news stories they know to be false or omit certain facts of a story to create a narrative which is usually driven by a political agenda. This term has become a part of our everyday lexicon, primarily by Donald Trump, when he ran for President of the United States and subsequently throughout his administration.

You don't have to be a news junkie to hear Mr. Trump call the latest scandal involving either himself or a member of his administration to be fake news. Whether it is the size of the crowd at his inauguration in January 2016, which he claimed were bigger than reported or the widely reported dysfunction of how the White House is operating—the term fake news is repeated over and over again to the point where people are confused as to what they should and should not believe.

This dividing force of facts versus fake news has crept into the church. We are living in a time where people in the religious community are preaching a "Gospel" that promotes White supremacy, Xenophobia and the justifying economic exploitation of the poor as doctrines and political positions that Jesus would approve of.

The reason why this book is titled, *We Gon' Be Alright: A Message of Hope for Believers in a God of Social Justice,* is to counter the false narrative of God being on the side of the rich and ruthless while forsaking the needs and necessities of the least and left out. Jesus made it clear in his inaugural sermon in **Luke 4:18-19** when he said: *"The Spirit of the Lord is upon me, because he has anointed me to proclaim good news to the poor. He has sent me to proclaim liberty to the captives and recovering of sight to the blind, to set at liberty those who are oppressed, to proclaim the year of the Lord's favor."* It is a shame that the true message of Christ is being politicized to the detriment of the very people He lived and died for.

It is my prayer that the messages in this book will empower and inspire a renewed urgency to embrace the true meaning of the Gospel of Jesus Christ. Not only that, but also reassure those who are experiencing what's going on locally, nationally and globally that God is still with us. God is still on our side and our God is a God of justice.

Psalm 37:28 states, *"For the Lord loves justice; he will not forsake his saints."* We must be reminded of this scripture when we see injustice in the world. Whether it's the killing of unarmed Black people by the police or the fact that study after study in this country shows that rent is too high for the poor in this country or when the president of the United States refers to nations populated by people of African descent as s—hole countries, we must stand up and speak truth to power with a confident "thus saith the Lord" on our lips.

This book is composed of sermons that were preached with an emphasis on the importance of social justice when proclaiming the Gospel of Jesus Christ. I deemed this book necessary because too much of the conversation around God and the present state of this country revolve around conservative theology that supports the status quo.

The timing of this book is very important. So many people are losing hope in God and humanity. In just a short span of time, we have witnessed so much hate-filled rhetoric in our public discourse. Some of that discourse has led to violent acts against fellow Americans and immigrants.

My prayer is that the messages in this book serve as reminders to all of God's children that these turbulent times have not come to stay, but they have come to pass. There is more that unites us than separates us. Jesus said these words in the Gospel of John 16:33, *"I have told you all this so that you may have peace in me. Here on earth you will have many trials and sorrows. But take heart, because I have overcome the world"* (NLT). It is because Jesus assured us that He has overcome the world that I take comfort in reminding you, that as a people and a nation, *We Gon' Be Alright!*

CHAPTER 1

"Trusting God During Trying Times"

Psalm 37:1-3

This chapter is centered on the premise that the providence of God can always be trusted. It is that trust that gives us peace during present difficult times while we wait for future deliverance. Our lives are always filled with times where it feels as if God is not near us or that we have been forgotten. The true mark of a believer is can we trust God?

As people of faith, we must also not let our commitment to social justice waver in the face of what we see every day. From abuses of power by the president and police to abusive policies by politicians, we know that God is with us, God is for us and most importantly God can be trusted.

Dr. Martin Luther King, Jr. on August 16, 1967, in his address to the Southern Christian Leadership Conference at their 10th annual convention, stated these words:

> **When our days become dreary with low-hovering**
> **clouds of despair, and when our nights become darker**
> **than a thousand midnights...Let us realize**
> **that the arc of the moral universe is long, but it bends**
> **toward justice.**

My sisters and brothers, I believe Dr. King is talking across the threshold of time and prophesying through the portal of the past to you and to me that what we are experiencing today has been experienced

1

before. That when the ruthless are ruling and it looks like the wicked are winning, we have to keep in mind the words of Dr. King that *moral arc of the universe is long, but it bends toward justice*; we must keep in mind the words of the psalmist that *weeping may endure for a night but joy comes in the morning*; we must keep in mind the words that our mothers and fathers sang, *I'm so glad that trouble don't last always!*

Let me take it back to the beginning in 2016 on 11/9 which Rev. Dr. Frederick Haynes III says was Black folks' 9/11, when the current occupant of the White House came into power after spending a year and a half reciting racist rhetoric while insulting and intimidating immigrants, appears on our television screens day after day continuing to do all that he can to tear this country apart.

It's gotten so bad that some of y'all don't even watch the news anymore. You're like "*Spann, I can't even turn it on. If I could, I would tell my cable provider to take CNN off of my plan and remove MSNBC from my package; if I could tell them what to do with Fox News and how to do it, I would!*"

It is very discouraging when you see children being stripped from their parents on our country's borders and the parents are imprisoned for trying to escape violence while the children are sent across the country wondering if they will ever see their parents again. Children as young as 18 months old were being shipped around and put in cages, all in an effort to dehumanize them and discourage other people of color from coming to this country.

We look at the recent decisions from the Supreme Court; decisions to continue to legalize barriers to prevent people from voting to the continuing assault on unions with the goal of eventually destroying them so that the rich can continue to get richer while workers have no voice in their treatment.

Oh, and by the way, police have not stopped shooting unarmed black men. For instance, Antwon Rose—17-year-old Black child shot in the back by a White police officer in East Pittsburgh. The officer has been charged with manslaughter and 3rd degree murder, but I'm not holding my breath for a conviction.

The rapper T.I. put it best when he said:

"They pull you over, ask you where your license at, Be careful reaching for it, you know you can die for that.

And this ain't nothing new, just got cameras so you can see [it]; Got Dr. King and Abe Lincoln askin' where the freedom at; This ain't no equality; Man, you ain't have no justice on your mind when you shot at me."[1]

Oh, but there is good news today! God has sent me here to remind you that no matter how much hell the wicked raise; no matter how the envious appear to be enjoying themselves; no matter how successful sinners seem to be, God wants you to know that their time is short and their reign is coming to an end quickly.

That is a reason to shout right there, because God has placed an expiration date on the schemes of the wicked. Just like that milk carton in your refrigerator, that loaf of bread in your pantry, that prescription for your medication—there's an expiration date, meaning after a certain date, it won't be good anymore, it can't be used, it won't be effective. In other words, once that date comes to pass, it will no longer be able to do what it was able to do before!

In today's text, David is wondering why God is allowing the wicked this time to reign and wreak havoc. But God reminds David (like He's doing to you and me) to trust Him and that the time of the wicked is coming to an end.

Let me give you the context to help you better appreciate the content.

Psalm 37 was written by King David. Y'all remember David, the young shepherd who slayed Goliath; the King and commander; the worshiper and the writer; the singer and psalmist. At this point in his life, he is an old man and he writes this Psalm as an acrostic poem, meaning each stanza starts with a letter from the Hebrew alphabet and it runs like that all the way to the end.

David, according to verse 25, is an old man, and he is wrestling with the age-old question, "Why do the righteous suffer while the wicked appear to prosper?" As you read the psalm, David reminds us that as

---

[1] Rapper and Activist TI *Warzone* Released 2016

Christians, we are called to take the long view. We cannot get caught up with the temporary and the transient. But we are called to *build our hopes on things eternal and hold to God's unchanging hand.* In other words, God—through David—is telling you and me *"Trust Me, I know what I'm doing!"*

Verse 1, *"Fret not yourself because of evil doers; be not envious of wrong doers!"* That word "fret" literally means to "burn" or to "kindle a flame" or become "hot." In other words, don't allow the schemes of the wicked to let you get angry and fuming and upset about what you're seeing in the world. Then David says, "And don't be envious or jealous of the wicked either."

In other words, we are living in times where it looks like the wicked are winning. A time where racists are using the police to serve as their personal racist valet service. If they see a Black person they believe to be out of place, the police will show up and do the bidding of these bigots while acting as instruments of intimidation instead of—let me give you another "I"—completing an investigation. They're supposed to ask questions of both sides instead of rolling up and immediately endorsing and empowering one side while embarrassing and sometimes emasculating the other.

Y'all know what I'm talking about: Black folks can't even sit in Starbucks anymore, can't even barbeque in the park; a Yale student can't even fall asleep on campus, and I saw this week, a 12-year-old boy can't even cut grass in peace!

But the Bible says, "Don't get mad, don't get upset but be cool." Know that God is in control; as a matter of fact, I'm in verse 2—the time of the wicked will be coming to an end shortly. The Bible describes the wicked as grass that fades away or is cut down and burned.

Have you ever seen something fade away? Have you ever had a shirt or a blouse or a pair of jeans and after washing them several times—that the dark blue turns to a lighter blue and then a lighter blue—that means its fading? Likewise, God is saying that some of the wicked will fade away, others will be cut down, and some will burn! The Bible didn't say this is going to take forever—but *they will soon fade like the grass and wither like the green herb.* That's why you cannot get angry at their antics or mad at their motives or lose your mind over their legislation—but be cool, because the Lord has assured you and He's assured me that their time is coming to an end.

So, Pastor what should we do in the meantime? I'm glad you asked. Look at verse 3 -*Trust in the Lord, and do good; dwell in the land and befriend faithfulness*. Let me unpack that a bit. **_Trust in the Lord_.** That word trust in the Hebrew is *batach* (baw-takh) which means to be confident or sure, to be bold. We ought to be confident and bold in the Lord during these times. Not hiding, not being *scurred*, not putting our heads in the sand, but trusting in the Lord.

Don't look at what's going on out here and doubt that God is not faithful, that God cannot be trusted. Remember, *we walk by faith, not by sight*[2].

Yes, it looks bad that Donald Trump will get to pick another Supreme Court justice; yes, it is bad that African-Americans are 12-13% of the US population yet African-Americans are incarcerated at more than 5 times the rate of Whites; yes, it is alarming watching brown children on our nation's borders snatched from the arms of their mothers and placed in cages with no plans for reunification. But, we still must trust in the Lord.

Not only does the text tell us to trust in the Lord but to **_do good._** In this season, we should be bold in the Lord and do good. We should speak up and speak out against injustice; keep ministering to the least and the left out; feeding the hungry and clothing the naked— *"And let us not be weary in well doing: for in due season we shall reap, if we faint not."*[3]

Then the text says, "*dwell in the land and befriend faithfulness*." Here, David encourages the people to stay where you are. Some people were tempted to leave the land, but God had promised them an inheritance in that land. If you leave the land then that can be interpreted as God is not faithful and that God cannot be trusted.

My sisters and brothers, I encourage you today to stay in the land. Stay where God has placed you. Don't pick up and leave because they're talking about you; don't walk off that job if God has not told you to; don't leave your family because of a disagreement; don't leave the church just because things aren't going your way right now. If God has not told you to leave, then you and I need to **_dwell in the land._** Ok, let me help you

---

[2] 2 Corinthians 5:7 *Holy Bible*

[3] Galatians 6:9, *Holy Bible*

out some more. *No, we're not going back to Africa!* Our ancestors <u>built and bled</u> for this country, we have <u>sacrificed and served</u> this country; we have <u>labored and loved</u> this country; I don't mean to <u>sour your celebration,</u> but we are going to dwell in the land! **<u>We're going to keep fighting for justice</u>**; keep standing up to the Orange one at 1600 Penn Ave; keep loving our children and respecting our elders. Just like we used to sing in the freedom movement, *"Well I'm on my way to heaven, We shall not be moved, On my way to heaven, We shall not be moved, Just like a tree that's planted by the waters, We shall not be moved!"*

Not only should we dwell in the land, but the Bible says, "***dwell in the land and befriend faithfulness.***" Another translation of that reads, *"Feed on His faithfulness."* During these times, we should not be caught up in what the wicked are doing but we should be feeding on God's faithfulness. We should embrace the fact that God is faithful.

The faithfulness of God is not based upon what I can see. <u>The Bible says that the just shall live by faith</u>[4]. Just because what I'm seeing right now doesn't line up with God's Word, does not mean that God is not faithful. It means that during this season, I should be feeding off what He's doing right now. He's been faithful in:

- Waking me up this morning and starting me on my way;
- Putting food on my table;
- Keeping a roof over my head;
- Keeping me from dangers seen and unseen.

David understood this concept when he lived like a fugitive, running from Saul. But God still kept him, until he finally sat upon the throne that God promised him. Has there ever been a time in your life where things were difficult, but God kept you through it all? He got you through those teenage years with your child; kept food on your table while you were unemployed; He kept you in your right mind as you went back and forth to the doctor. Touch your neighbor and tell them, *"Feed off of His faithfulness."*

My sisters and brothers, God is faithful. The providence of God

---

[4] Romans 1:17 *Holy Bible*

can always be trusted. It is that trust that gives us peace during present difficult times while we wait for future deliverance.

Just imagine what your life would be like if you trusted God through your trying times. Instead of gazing at our problem and glancing at God, flip that thing around and rather gaze at God while occasionally glancing at your problem. You will know that our God is faithful and that our God can be trusted.

I'll leave you with this as I take my seat:

One-day, the great preacher and theologian, Charles Spurgeon, was walking through the English countryside with a friend. As they strolled along, the evangelist noticed a barn with a weather vane on its roof. At the top of the weather vane were these words: "GOD IS LOVE." So, Spurgeon says to his companion that he thought this was a rather inappropriate place for such a message. *"Weather vanes are changeable,"* he said, *"but God's love is constant."* So, Spurgeon's friend says, *"I don't agree with you about those words, Charles."* He goes on to say, *"You misunderstand the meaning. That sign is indicating a truth: Regardless of which way the wind blows, God is love."*

And that's all I stopped by to tell you today, that no matter which way the winds blow in your life, God is love. No matter which way the winds blow, God can be trusted. No matter which way the winds blow, God is faithful! No matter which way the winds blow, God is still working on your behalf!

The winds and the storms of life will blow in our lives, but the Good News is that through it all God is with us. The songwriter puts it this way:

> *Though the storms keep on raging in my life, And sometimes it's hard to tell the night from day...But if the storms don't cease, And if the winds keep on blowing in my life, My soul has been anchored in the Lord!*

CLOSING PRAYER

Dear God, during this season of social unrest and uncivil discourse, help those of us who believe in Your consistency and Your character to trust you. It can be difficult, because what we see does not always line up with what your Word says. Our minds at times wander into hopelessness and disbelief; our hearts at times become weary and worn; and even our commitment to the cause of righteousness and justice can become inconsistent. It is during these times, we ask for You to pour out a double portion of your anointing upon us and give us the strength and courage to continue in the fight. It is our prayer that we will never again give into doubt but when those thoughts come, let them depart from our minds just as quickly as they arose. You have not given us the spirit of fear, so let us not succumb nor succor to its intentions. But let us meet fear and doubt with faith. Faith in Your Word and faith in Your promises.
In Jesus name we pray, Amen.

CHAPTER 1 - REFLECTION QUESTIONS

1. In what areas of my life do I need to trust God?
2. What issues of social justice have I given up hope on?
3. Why is it important to trust God during trying times?

CHAPTER 2

"Don't Worry: Stick to the Plan"

God never intended for His children to worry. During these times
of political and personal unrest God is calling all of us to follow
His plan for inner peace while the wicked temporarily prosper.

Psalm 37:4-7

As many of you know, I coach my son's basketball team and while
I enjoy watching these young men develop, one of the greatest
challenges I have as a coach is getting them to stick to the game plan. We
practice regularly, we go over how we're going to play defense, we go over
our offense, and we go over how we're going to inbound the ball. But for
some reason, every now and then when things get difficult in the game,
if the other team makes a run or we find ourselves down, we abandon
the game plan; everybody starts doing their own thing and the next
thing we know, we've turned a manageable problem into a hot mess! It
was the legendary boxer Mike Tyson who once said that everybody has
a plan until you get hit!

Has that ever happened in your life? You've been coming to church
on a regular basis, haven't missed Bible Study, you say your prayers every
day; then the next thing you know—**Boom**—your life gets hit hard. **One
commercial says, "Life comes at you fast!"** Boom—you just lost your job;
Boom—a loved one dies—**Boom** your doctor finds something on your x-ray.

The next thing you know, you stopped coming to church, start
missing Bible Study, and stopped reading your Bible; the next thing

you know, you're telling yourself, "I just need something to help me unwind; I'm just drinking this to help me relax; I'm just smoking this to just clear my thoughts." Then the next thing you know, the saints haven't seen you in a few months. You start saying stuff like, "*I'm tired of church folk; they talk too much; I don't want them all in my business; they're too judgmental.*"

Now you're back hanging with your old friends and they're putting old thoughts back into your head—"*Girl, remember when we used to go to the Go-Go?*" (*Chuck Brown-rip-and Rare Essence...*) or "*Man, we used to get tore up all night*" or "*Oh, girl, remember so-and-so, yes he's still fine and he remembers you...*" Now you're trying to cuss to fit in and the cuss words don't flow the way they used to. And, you're trying to go back in—to that which God has pulled you out of—all because you didn't stick to the plan!

Don't get me wrong, this world will make it hard for you to stick to the plan, especially when you see the occupant of the White House tell the Justice Department to roll back the previous administration's guidelines on Affirmative Action. The comedian Chris Rock tells the joke, "*I've never been on a college campus and said there are not enough White people here.*" Then to top it off, this administration says that they are just applying the rule of law.

My sisters and brothers don't get fooled by that language. Just because something is legal, doesn't make it right. Remember, **Slavery** was legal. **Imprisoning people on our borders and taking their children** was legal. The **Japanese internment** was legal. The **Holocaust** was legal. The **Crucifixion** of Jesus was legal! Dr. King said, "An unjust law is no law at all."

We are living in a time where being Black is under attack. It seems as if every week we see the police being used to harass us in our everyday lives. We saw a woman this week in Oregon, who happened to be a State representative running for re-election, who was going door-to-door campaigning when someone called the police on her. Then in Maryland, a priest threw a Black family out of the funeral of their loved one. He had the nerve to tell them to "Get out of my church." Really, your church? I thought Jesus said, "**Upon this Rock I build My church!**"

That's why I was so glad, on the 4th of July, to see that sister, Patricia Okoumou climb the Statute of Liberty, then sit down and cross her legs, to let America know that we're not going anywhere and I'm going to sit on Lady Liberty's robe and hold her in place so that this nation lives up to what it put down on paper as being "one nation, under God, indivisible with liberty and justice for all!"

My sisters and brothers, thanks be to God that there is no need to worry. God has given you and I a plan on how to triumph in a "Trumped" world. I like what God does here in **Psalm 37**. His plan focuses on us getting ourselves right on the inside so that we can handle what's happening on the outside. I must make sure my internal posture will influence my external praxis. Lauren Hill said it best, *"How you gon' win when you ain't right within?"* We are in a time where God wants us to walk in wisdom and not worry.

Let me give you the context to help you better appreciate the content.

Psalm 37 is written by King David. Y'all remember David, the young shepherd and psalmist, the King and commander, the worshiper and the warrior. At this point in his life, he is an old man. He writes this Psalm as an acrostic poem, meaning each stanza starts with a letter from the Hebrew alphabet and it runs like that all the way to the end.

David, according to verse 25, is an old man and he is wrestling with the age-old question, "Why do the righteous suffer while the wicked appear to prosper." As you read the Psalm, David reminds us that as Christians, we are called to take the long view. As Christians, we are not just called to live for the future, but we are called to live by the future as well. We must grasp that we **walk by faith, not by sight.** Paul also said in Romans 8:18, *"For I consider that the sufferings of this present time are not worth comparing with the glory that is to be revealed to us."*

In today's text, David tells us not to worry, because everything will work out if we stick to the plan. Let me give you the 3 steps to the plan:

1. We must **Delight in the Lord**—**Verse 4,** *"Delight yourself in the Lord, and he will give you the desires of your heart."* The word "delight" in the Hebrew comes from a root word that means "to be brought up in luxury, to be pampered." It speaks to the abundance of God's blessings that we have in God Himself,

apart from what He gives. In other words, I am to be more consumed with the Blessor than the blessing. You and I have got to realize that it doesn't matter what we are going through, God doesn't change. The songwriter said, *"The world is ever changing but you are still the same."* David puts it this way in Psalm 34, *"I will bless the Lord at all times and His praises shall continually be in my mouth"*

God is saying to you (and to me) that this is the season to be consumed with Him. Yes, things are not going the way you planned; Yes, it would be nice to have more money in my bank account; Yes, our government has been hijacked by hatred leaving many in misery because of a lack of morality, but I believe today that God is using our current events to correct the compass of our hearts and to get us back to looking to Him, loving Him and ultimately living for Him!

Verse 4 *"Delight yourself in the Lord, and he will give you the desires of your heart."* The second part of that verse says, *"...and he will give you the desires of your heart."* The word "desires" is translated as "desire or petition." In other words, once I delight in the Lord that will open the doors to what I've been praying for.

Sisters and Brothers, maybe your blessings are being blocked and your help is on hold, not because of your actions but by where you've set your affection. God knows that if He gives you your desire or petition that you'll thank Him, tell Him to take a seat over there, and "I'll take it from here." We can't love stuff more than the Savior. We can't want money more than the Messiah. We must never put a job over Jesus.

God wants to bless us so badly that He said if you just delight in Me, I'll give you the desires of your heart. You won't have to work for it. You won't have to be up all day and night for it. You won't lose any sleep over it. God said, "I'll give you your desire if you delight in Me!"

2. Not only must we delight in the Lord, but we must **Depend on the Lord**—**Verses 5-6,** *"Commit your way to the Lord; trust in him, and he will act. He will bring forth your righteousness as the light, and your justice as the noonday."* The word "commit" means "to roll off your burdens." God wants us to commit to

rolling over or turning our burdens over to Him. **1 Peter 5:6-7** puts it better, *"Humble yourselves, therefore, under the mighty hand of God so that at the proper time he may exalt you, casting all your anxieties on him, because he cares for you."*

God is saying to you (and to me) that during these times of crises and chaos, the way to not worry and stick to the plan is to make a concentrated effort to turn my problems and my burdens over to the Lord. The old church hymn says:

> *If you trust and never doubt, He will surely bring you out, Take your burdens to the Lord and leave them there.*

Then the text says, *"Trust in Him and He will act."* We talked about trusting in Him last week. Here, the text says that if we trust in Him He will act. **Are y'all starting to see the benefits of sticking to the plan?** Verse 4 told us that if we delight in Him, He'll give us the desires of our hearts and now in verse 5 we are told that if we give Him our burdens and trust in Him, He will act on our behalf. If you want God to act, then you'll have to give Him your burdens.

You see there can't be 2 gods at work at the same time. Either you're going to handle it or God's going to handle it. God is not going to fight with you for your problem. He'll fight for you, but He won't fight with you. We must trust God and His timing so that He can act on our behalf.

Verse 6 says, *"He will bring forth your righteousness as the light, and your justice as the noonday."* God will vindicate you. You don't have to worry about getting back at your co-worker; don't waste your time proving your cousin wrong; you don't have to post pictures on Instagram trying to show your ex how they messed up by letting you go. Romans 12:19 says, *"Beloved, never avenge yourselves, but leave it to the wrath of God, for it is written, 'Vengeance is mine, I will repay, says the Lord.'"*

The text says that He will bring forth your righteousness and your justice. My heart breaks every time I see videos of police brutality, or assaults against immigrant communities or how laws are passed to take away our voting rights. However, I believe that if we continue to trust in the Lord, He will bring forth both our righteousness and our justice.

3. We must stay **Disciplined in the plan of God**. **Verse 7 says,** *"Be still before the Lord and wait patiently for him; fret not yourself over the one who prospers in his way, over the man who carries out evil devices!"* **The first part of that verse tells us to be still and wait patiently for the Lord.**

Sometimes the hardest thing in life is to be still and to be patient. Especially when you <u>want</u> to do something and you <u>feel</u> like you <u>should</u> be doing something. Remember, God doesn't want us to fret. Remember from last week, fret means "to kindle a flame or to get hot." This is because when you get hot you can make bad decisions.

<u>Remember, that's how Moses got into trouble</u>. He saw one of those Egyptians messing with one of his fellow Hebrews and he jumped up and killed the man, forcing him to go on the run and get put on Egypt's Most Wanted list. He's forced to the life of a fugitive. God has him living on the backside of the desert for 40 years until He calls Moses back to Egypt. Now, had Moses been patient and waited to do it God's way—God didn't want to liberate the Hebrews that way—things could have turned out differently for him, because many times God's method's are different from ours. Instead, Moses got upset, got heated, began to fret and got out of the will of God.

One of the most transformative moments in the civil rights movement happened on February 1, 1960 in Greensboro, NC. Four Students at North Carolina A&T named, Ezell Blair Jr., David Richmond, Franklin McCain and Joseph McNeil decided to do a sit-in during the time of segregation at a Woolworth's lunch counter. It was Joseph McNeil who suggested the sit-in. To McNeil, discipline in executing the protest was paramount. Months before the sit-in, he attended a concert at which other African-American students behaved carelessly, leaving him determined not to repeat their error.

So, the four men went and sat at the Woolworth's lunch counter and requested service. They were refused service, but sat there until it closed. Still, they were refused service. So, they kept coming back, and more and more students came with them. Then the next thing you know, this sit-in movement spread all over the country. By the end of March, the movement had spread to 55 cities in 13 States.

Now, it wasn't all peaceful. In some places, students were surrounded by White counter-protestors and they were spit on and assaulted, and someone's coat was even set on fire. But through it all, they stayed disciplined.

In response to the success of the sit-in movement, dining facilities across the South were being integrated by the summer of 1960. At the end of July, when many local college students were on summer vacation, the Greensboro Woolworth's quietly integrated its lunch counter.

I know it's difficult to daily look at the viciousness and vanity of the wicked, because, truth be told, the wicked are prospering. They are having the time of their lives right now. But like the Greensboro 4, we must be disciplined. We must be focused and not fret; have faith and not fear; have hope and not lose heart!

God never intended for His children to worry. During these times of political and personal unrest, God is calling all of us to follow His plan for inner peace while the wicked temporarily prosper.

This week, I want you to write down the three top things that you are worrying about. No one has to know. You can write them out and then throw away the list. But make a determination that you're going to stick to the plan that this week you will delight in the Lord, depend on the Lord and be disciplined in the Lord.

Just imagine what your life would be like if you declared your life a worry-free zone. If you made up your mind to stick to the plan that no matter what comes your way, you're staying in the Word of God, in the way of God and in the will of God!

In the summer Olympics, one of the lesser-known sports featured is rowing. Rowing consists of nine men on a boat. Now, eight of the men are big, strong men whose job it is to use the oars and row the boat. Oh and one thing, these eight men, while rowing, sit with their backs to the finish line. The 9th man is called, "the coxswain." The coxswain might be the most important man on the boat, because he sits at the front of the boat facing the finish line. It's his job to make sure everyone is safe, that the boat is being maneuvered properly, to coach the crew, to encourage and motivate them, to make all the tactical decisions and to tell them when to speed up and when to slow down.

The guys in the boat keep their eyes fixed on the coxswain while they row. While they can't see the finish line, he can. So, they keep their eyes fixed on him.

People of God, if you're worried about where your life is going, if you're worried that all your labor is in vain; if you're worried that all your action will have no effect on the wicked—I need you to keep your eyes fixed on Jesus, because He sees where the finish line is.

Don't worry, stick to the plan. Trust that God knows where you're going. He knows when you'll get there and He knows how to get you there.

Don't worry, God's got you.

- He's keeping you from dangers seen and unseen
- He's leading you through the valley of the shadow of death
- He's a very present help in time of trouble
- Don't worry, stick to the plan

Gospel singer Anthony Brown reminds to keep our eyes on God when he sings:

You did not create me to worry, You did not create me to fear, But You created me to worship daily, So I'mma leave it all right here...I will trust in You, trust in You, Lord I will put my trust in You, I will put my trust in You.

Do you trust Him today? Will you Trust Him today? Yes, I will trust You Lord!

CLOSING PRAYER

Lord Jesus, help me not to worry during this season of my life. Give me Your peace that surpasses all understanding. Help me to keep my eyes on You when the days are long, and the nights are dark. Lord, I need your help in keeping my eyes on my calling. I claim your peace and your presence during this time. In Jesus' name, Amen.

CHAPTER 2 - REFLECTION QUESTIONS

1. In what areas of your life do you need to be more disciplined?
2. What area of your life do you need to turn over to the Lord?
3. List what you believe that keeps distracting you from sticking to the plan of God? How do you plan to eliminate the distractions?

CHAPTER 3

"After This"

God does not want us to be angry during this season.
For another season is coming. In His Word, God has
guaranteed the downfall of the wicked after this season.

Psalm 37:8-11

This past week, many of us, much like the rest of the world, watched as the 45th president of the U.S., both literally and deliberately, chose to side with Vladimir Putin, the current president of Russia. We all know that Russia has been an enemy of the United States for at least the last um...70 years! How could it be that when confronted with evidence from all 17 U.S. intelligence agencies that Russia indeed interfered with our last presidential election, 45 still chose to believe the word of Putin than his own country?

To hear the president of this country, beside the fact that most of us Americans (nearly 3 million) did not vote for him, literally side with one of our major enemies is enough to take you from **huh** to **what** to **you've got to be kidding me** to **full blown anger**. On top of that, this current Congress is looking to allow him to pick another Supreme Court Justice! Marvin Gaye would say, "*It makes me wanna holler, the way they do my life.*"

Don't it make you wanna holler that **children are still at the border in cages**, separated from their parents? Don't it make you wanna holler that there is **still no clean water in Flint**, Michigan? Don't it make you wanna holler that unarmed Black people are still being shot and killed by the police!

Isn't it frustrating that the issue of police brutality is as old as the police department itself? We know that policing goes back to the slave patrols, where laws were put in place to control the slave population and protect the interest of slave owners. So, you had these fugitive slave laws that included the detention and return of runaway slaves.

Over the years, we've seen how society has used police to control and punish Black people at every twist and turn. We now see the police being called on Black people for just minding their own business. It's become so crazy that the Internet has given these folks names like Permit Patty, in San Francisco. She called the police on an 8-year old Black girl who was selling water in front of her building to raise money for a trip to Disneyland, because her mom lost her job.

Then there was Barbeque Becky in Oakland who called the police on two Black men who were grilling with a charcoal grill in the park. Just several days ago, we had Coupon Carl, a CVS manager in Chicago, who called the police on a Black woman for allegedly using a fake coupon. While the woman was simply trying to use a coupon from the manufacturer, in an interesting twist of fate, Coupon Carl had been busted for forgery less than 2 years ago.

We see time and time again how Whites have called the police on Blacks, for the most trivial of matters, knowing that the slightest interaction between the police and a Black man, or the police and a Black woman, or the police and a Black boy or girl, could end up being fatal for that African-American. In other words, many in our society have decided that White comfort is more important than Black existence. Actually, a White person's comfort trumps (for lack of a better word) whether or not a Black person lives or dies.

I don't know about you, but that statement or thought is enough to make your blood boil, make your temperature rise, and make you want to **lose your mind up in here, up in here**!

The great writer and activist James Baldwin once said, *"To be a Negro in this country and to be relatively conscious is to be in a rage almost all the time."*

While the times should both make us angry and move us to action, there is good news today in the Word of God that demonstrates to you and to me that God doesn't want us operating out of anger during this season. Yes, the wicked are winning and evil is empowered, but today's text teaches us that we don't have to waste our time with anger, because this era is not eternal. This administration is not almighty and the rule of evil is not endless.

There is a time when the <u>righteous will rise</u>, the <u>called will conquer</u> and the <u>royal priesthood will take its rightful place</u>. A time when we will come to know:

- <u>Romans 8:18</u> - *that our present sufferings are not worth comparing with the glory that will be revealed in us;*
- <u>1 Peter 5:10</u> - *And the God of all grace, who called you to his eternal glory in Christ, after you have suffered a little while, will himself restore you and make you strong, firm and steadfast;*
- <u>Isaiah 40:31</u> - *But they that wait upon the Lord shall renew their strength; they shall mount up with wings as eagles; they shall run, and not be weary; and they shall walk, and not faint.*

In today's text, God shows us that the time of wickedness will come to an end and that we will be rewarded <u>after this!</u>

<u>Let me give you the context of the text to help you better appreciate the content.</u>

We know that Psalm 37 is written by David in his old age. It is during this Psalm that he wrestles with the age-old question, "<u>Why do bad things happen to good people</u>?" David is trying to invigorate his intellect, while searching his spirituality all to try to come to a conclusion to the matter.

While David is searching this matter, God reveals to him in verse 8 to not get angry. Verse 8: *"Refrain from anger, and forsake wrath! Fret not yourself; it tends only to evil."* God is telling David to loosen or relax and let go of your anger.

I believe God is sending the same message to you and me today to let go of our anger. <u>Yes,</u> you should be angry when you see <u>videos of police</u>

brutality. <u>Yes,</u> you should be angry where <u>every day the prices for food and housing go up, yet wages stay the same</u>. <u>Yes,</u> we should be angry when this city, Washington, D. C., can make provisions to <u>build 2 sports stadiums just blocks from here</u>, yet so many people in this neighborhood are in poverty and can't even afford to go to the games.

The Bible is clear by telling us to let it go. ***"Refrain from anger, and forsake wrath!"*** Now understand anger has its place. **Ephesians 4:26-27 says, *"Be angry and do not sin; do not let the sun go down on your anger, and give no opportunity to the devil."*** If I allow myself to operate solely from a place of anger, for too long, it can control me and give way to the devil. Don't get me wrong, anger can sometimes be a great place to start. Many of you never stood up for yourself until you got angry. It took you getting angry to leave that bad relationship or leave that bad job. Many times, anger has birthed many marches, movements and organizations.

"Refrain from anger and forsake wrath! Fret not yourself; it tends only to evil." The word, "evil," here in Hebrew means "to spoil or break into pieces or to make good for nothing." If I allow current events or even my current situation to allow me to dwell in anger, it can ruin me, spoil me, or make me good for nothing for the next season of my life. God is saying to you and to me that if we do not allow anger to have the last say in our lives that there will be deliverance from the wicked after this season. Allow me to break it down like this:

1. God promised to deliver us from the **Power** of the wicked. Verse 9: ***"For the evildoers shall be cut off, but those who wait for the Lord shall inherit the land."*** In the next season, the wicked will not have power over you. Yes, the powers that be look insurmountable. It looks like they're in every office of government; it looks like they have all the money and are aligned with all the powerful people. However, we serve a God that used a shepherd boy and five smooth stones to slay a giant. He used a staff to part the Red Sea. He used a carpenter's son to heal the sick and raise people from the dead.

Yes, the wicked are powerful, but we serve a God who is all-powerful! The scriptures tell us: *Now unto Him who is able to do exceeding and abundantly above all that we can ask think or even imagine.*[5]

---

[5] Ephesians 3:20, *Holy Bible*

2. God promises to deliver us from the **Penalty** of the wicked. *"For the evildoers shall be cut off, but those who wait for the Lord shall inherit the land."* Yes, the same land that the wicked is using, God will turn it around for you and for me. There is power in patience. Waiting for the Lord doesn't mean we sit by with our arms folded waiting for a miracle to happen. Instead, we watch and pray. Like Nehemiah, when they were rebuilding the wall, we have a tool to build in one hand and a weapon in the other.

3. Lastly, God will deliver us from the very **Presence** of the wicked. Verses 10-11: *"In just a little while, the wicked will be no more; though you look carefully at his place, he will not be there. But the meek shall inherit the land and delight themselves in abundant peace."*

The Bible went so far to say that we'll look carefully at his (the wicked's) place and he won't be there. Now understand, David is speaking about those in the community who will be cut out and removed and, in some instances, executed. God is serious about removing evil from the land of promise.

The last verse should be very familiar. *"But the meek shall inherit the land and delight themselves in abundant peace."* Jesus quotes this text in **Matthew 5:5** when He says, *"Blessed are the meek, for they shall inherit the earth..."*

The Bible speaks of the "meek" that doesn't imply that they are weak. Biblical Commentator Warren Wiersbe calls meekness a force under the control of faith. Have folks ever mistaken your meekness for weakness? They spread all kind of lies and you won't respond; messing with you on the job, messing with you in your home. All the while, they don't know it's taking everything in you not to go off! God is telling you and me that if we walk in meekness and don't allow anger to rule us, then we will see His deliverance!

God does not want us to be controlled by anger during this season. In His Word, God has guaranteed the downfall of the wicked after this season. God has guaranteed the downfall of your haters and naysayers.

This week, just start praising God for keeping you right now and for what He's about to do. Tell Him, "Lord I praise You (I thank You, I love You) for what You're going to do after this!"

Just imagine how much more peace you would have if you keep reminding yourself that there is something greater for me after this.

- God will fix my life—after this
- God will open doors of opportunity—after this
- God will surround me with people who love me—after this
- God will heal my heart from this hurt –after this
- God will restore my credit—after this
- God will take this spirit of depression off of me—after this
- <u>God has promised me my inheritance—after this</u>

The gospel recording artist JJ Harriston says:

There will be glory after this.
There will be victory after this.
God will turn it around,
He will bring you out.
There will be glory after this.

<u>Is that your testimony today?</u>

CLOSING PRAYER

Dear God, as one who is a lover of social justice, help me in this season to not allow my disdain for injustice to cloud my judgment. Help me to keep my emotions in check. Give me the divine revelation that weeping may endure for a night, but joy comes in the morning. Lord I know your timing is perfect. Help me to keep working for freedom, justice, and equality even when it looks like my labor is in vain. Remind me daily that my labor is never in vain when I'm serving You. In Jesus' name, I pray, Amen.

CHAPTER 3 - REFLECTION QUESTIONS

1. How can you harness your righteous indignation against the wicked to work for you and not against you?
2. What does it mean in Ephesians 4:26-27, "Be angry and do not sin; do not let the sun go down on your anger, and give no opportunity to the devil?"
3. Can anger ever be used in a positive way for change?

CHAPTER 4

"We Gon' Be Alright"

Psalm 37:12-18

God's plan is always greater than every attack against
our community. Always keep in mind that God's got
us and the days of the wicked are numbered.

On June 30, 2015, Rapper, songwriter and yes, Pulitzer Prize winner, representing Compton, CA as a combination of both consciousness and creativity, Kendrick Lamar released the 4th single from his album, "To Pimp A Butterfly." The single simply titled, "Alright," has won Kendrick many accolades in the music industry from MTV Video Awards to BET Awards to two Grammy Awards.

Most importantly, the song has become an anthem to a generation that not only loves Hip-Hop, but also loves Social Justice. Many groups leading protests against police brutality, including Black Lives Matter, could be heard singing or playing this song. Kendrick Lamar has called it a song about hope.

I'm not going to give it all to you today, but I like what Kendrick does at the end of each verse. He says:

> *When you know we been hurt, been down before, n***a*
> *When my pride was low, lookin' at the world like,*
> *where do we go, n***a?*
> *And we hate Popo, wanna kill us dead in the street for*
> *sure, n***a*

I'm at the preacher's door
My knees gettin' weak and my gun might blow but we
gon' be alright

Here, Kendrick Lamar embraces and embodies the heartaches and the hardships that many in our community endure on a daily basis. **When you know, we been hurt, been down before, n***a. When my pride was low, lookin' at the world like, where do we go, n***a?** Yes Kendrick, we've been hurt and yes, we've been down before; like millions of our ancestors crossing the Atlantic Ocean, **enduring the middle passage in chains on our way to a strange land**. We know on August 20, 1619 in Jamestown, Port Comfort, VA, the first 20 enslaved Africans arrived in America. Yes*, we been hurt, been down before,* forced into 246 years of chattel slavery, our ancestors worked from can't see in the morning until can't see at night.

We fought in the Civil War and then anxiously awaited the signing of the Emancipation Proclamation on January 1, 1863. A short time after was the ratification of the 13th amendment, which outlawed slavery but left the caveat that gives an exception to those in jail, which we now see has opened the door for the mass incarceration crisis that is destroying Black and Brown communities to this day.

Then, we know that Reconstruction ends in 1877. We come to the Great Compromise when Rutherford B. Hayes becomes president and federal troops are pulled out of the South. Now with no federal protection in the South, the door opens up for Jim Crow to move in. Then, for nearly 100 years, legalized segregation in every area of life, to public transportation to public schools, to public places including restrooms and restaurants, were allowed to thrive under the legal precedent and social customs of separate but equal.

Then, we fast forward to the 1960's, in which we get the Civil Rights Act of 1964 that prohibited discrimination in areas like public facilities, public education, and public accommodations. Then, we get the Voting Rights Act of 1965, which prohibited the denial and restrictions on the right to vote. Then, we had the Fair Housing Act of 1968, which prohibited against the discrimination of the sale, financing, or rental of housing because of race. And we haven't even gotten to the 1970's!

Yes, we know what it's like to struggle as a people and as a group and community to try to make our lives better.

When you know, we been hurt, been down before, n***a
When my pride was low, lookin' at the world like, where do we go, n***a?

I like how Kendrick shifts from the people to the person. Has your pride ever been low, looking at the world like where do I go?

I'm talking about when your money gets funny and your change gets strange; when your credit can't get it; when your outgo exceeds your income, therefore leading to your upkeep becoming your downfall. I'm talking about making a decision to pay my doctor's co-pay or get groceries; deciding between my prescription or my rent; can I keep my cell phone on or pay my car note.

I'm talking about when times get difficult and you have no one to lean on. You've been there for everybody else's crises, but the minute you have a crisis, no one's around and nobody responds to your text; you can't get a call back—we all know what it's like to be there for others and then turn around in our own time of need and wonder where will my help come from.

There is good news today! God sent me here to remind you that *"We Gon' Be Alright!"* Every now and then, you need somebody to remind you that the Bible says, "Our *God is a very present help in time of trouble; that when the enemy comes in like a flood, our God will raise up a standard."* Or, sometimes we need Big Momma to remind us that *"I'm so glad that trouble don't last always."* We need Granddaddy to remind us that *"He may not come when you want Him, but He's always right on time!"*

That's why I love today's text, because David reminds you and me that God promised, "We Gon' Be Alright."

Let me help you out. Verse 12 states, *"The wicked plots against the righteous and gnashes his teeth at him, (verse 13) but the Lord laughs at the wicked, for he sees that his day is coming."*

Notice the wicked plots. In other words, they didn't wake up this morning wanting to get you, they've been plotting! They've been watching you, listening to you, figuring out what they can use against you, or whom they can turn against you. Sometimes I think about the haters in my life and wonder, "If you would spend this much time planning your own life, maybe things might be different for you!"

The wicked plots. But look at verse 13, *"But the Lord laughs at the wicked, for he sees that his day is coming."* Every now and then, you need to remind yourself that, yes, the wicked are plotting; yes, the haters are planning; yes, the backstabbers are positioning themselves—But God! That's a reason to shout right there!

This Bible that we believe, this chapter that we've chosen and these verses that we're viewing says, *"The wicked plots against the righteous and gnashes his teeth at him, but the Lord laughs at the wicked, for he sees that his day is coming."*

Every now and then, you need a "But God" praise. I know somebody here today can look back over your life and declare, "But God!" The doctors counted you out "But God"; You almost walked out on your marriage, "But God"; You never thought that your child or grandchild was going to get right, "But God"; You thought you were going to die with that diagnosis (but its 5 years later) "But God!"

The Bible tells us that while the wicked are lying, God is laughing; while the wicked are scheming, God is smiling; while the wicked are colluding, God is chuckling. Why? Because *He knows his day is coming!*

My sisters and brothers, just like you and I can't see what God has for us on the other side of our trials, the wicked can't see what God has for them on the other side of their triumphs! They're celebrating giving tax breaks to the rich, excited about dismantling healthcare and they're throwing the collusion in our face by meeting with Putin and saying we may have another meeting in Washington or in Moscow—But God—He's looking at His watch laughing, because He knows [the wicked's] day is coming!

The word "day" in the Hebrew here is translated *Yom* which means "day, daylight or a specific moment in time." In other words, God knows when the wicked's time is coming to an end, just like He knows when your breakthrough is coming. While the wicked are wreaking havoc, God is checking His watch. While the wicked are sowing corruption,

God is staring at His clock. While the wicked are spreading terror, God is checking His timer. God always knows what time it is.

When you know, we been hurt, been down before, n***a
When my pride was low, lookin' at the world like, where do we go,
n***a?
And we hate Popo, wanna kill us dead in the street for sure, n***a

Above, we see Kendrick Lamar dealing with the systemic forces that are used to oppress his people.

Look at verse 14—*The wicked draw the sword and bend their bows to bring down the poor and needy, to slay those whose way is upright.* Look at all of the strength and might used to bring down the poor and needy. Look at how our communities are over policed. Look at how rampant violence is against African-Americans; how the actor Ving Rhames talked about having a gun pulled on him while in his own home (good for him that the police chief recognized him, it could have gone the other way). The NFL still wants to tell Black men when and where to protest. Help me understand this, if you can tell me where to protest, when to protest and how to protest, is it really a protest?

Sadly, in California, a young sister, 18-year-old Nia Wilson, was stabbed to death by a White man while she was waiting for a train. It feels as if every day there's one racially motivated attack after another, some senseless killing in our community after another, some scandal by our government one after another and one reckless tweet after another.

We feel like we are in the midst of a psychologically torturous Groundhogs Day, where we keep reliving the same trauma, watching the same images of Black suffering over and over and again.

I love verse 16— *Better is the little that the righteous has than the abundance of many wicked.*

We spend so much time wanting what the wicked has. Now don't get me wrong, every person that has money is not wicked. There's nothing wrong with wanting wealth or going out and getting it. What the Bible is talking about here concerns those who have gained their abundance through ungodly ways – those who profit off of healthcare to the point that poor people can't afford treatment or prescription drugs. Yes, we're talking about those who profit off of war, who build weapons of war and encourage our government to war so that they can profit. We're talking about lobbyists like the NRA who will pay legislators to keep automatic weapons on the street after witnessing all of these mass shootings and misuse the Constitution to support their twisted logic.

God is trying to tell us that what little we have is more valuable than the gains of the wicked, because what we have is eternal. Remember, the wicked's day is coming. What we have the world didn't give it to us and the world can't take it away. That's why we need to listen to the old church choir when they used to sing:

> *Silver and gold, Silver and gold*
> *I'd rather have Jesus than silver and gold*
> *No fame or fortune*
> *Nor riches untold*
> *I'd rather have Jesus than silver and gold*

God reminds us that what we have is eternal, what we have will still be here once the wicked are cut off and what we have can never be taken from us.

God's plan is always greater than whatever the enemy is plotting. Always keep in mind that God's got us and the days of the wicked are numbered.

This week remind yourself that we gone be alright. My **family** is going to be alright; my **church** is going to be alright; my **neighborhood's** gon' be alright; the **Black community** is going to be alright—because *I got a feeling everything's gonna be alright, I got a feelin' everything's gonna be alright. The Holy Ghost done told me everything's gonna be alright!*

> *I'm at the preacher's door*
> *My knees gettin' weak and my gun might blow but we*
> *gon' be alright*

Verse 18 says, *"For the arms of the wicked shall be broken, but the Lord upholds the righteous."* God says here that the arms of the wicked, the defenses of the wicked, that which the wicked would use to break their fall, will be broken. It appears as if the righteous are defenseless, but it's really the wicked. When their day comes it's over.

But the Lord upholds the righteous. God keeps us strong and He keeps us upright when we feel down. God gives us that strength when we feel weak and He gives us protection when we feel powerless.

<u>Let me try to illustrate this</u>: Years ago, we were living in Laurel, Maryland and our neighbor had a basketball hoop (we got one later) at the time. My son, Peter II, had to have been around 6 or 7 and he would shoot on the neighbor's rim. I remember one day I was working on a sermon or something and he runs in the house and says, "Dad, I can dunk." I said, "Boy, get out of here, stop playing." And he says, "No, Dad, I can dunk." Now, you have to understand that this rim is at regulation height or close to it.

So, I finally get up and cut across the grass to my neighbor's hoop. I walk up and I'm like, "Let me see." So, Peter says, "Let me show you I can dunk." He picks up the ball, backs into me and says, "Lift me up!"

That's what I need somebody here to understand this morning that—*the arms of the wicked shall be broken, but the Lord upholds the righteous.*

- When it looks like you can't make it, God will lift you up
- When you feel like you can't take it, God will lift you up
- When your self-esteem gets low, God will lift you up
- When you want to throw in the towel God will lift you up
- When you're weak in your body, God will lift you up
- When you feel like you can't go on, God will lift you up
- When the chips are stacked against you, God will lift you up

Just hold to His hand, God's unchanging hand and build your hopes on things eternal and keep holding to God's unchanging hand!

I need somebody to know today that We Gon' Be Alright!

- They can flood our community with drugs, but we gon' be alright
- Break up our families through mass incarceration, but we gon' be alright
- Shoot and kill unarmed Black men, but we gon' be alright
- They drive down wages for working people, but we gon' be alright
- Do everything you can to gentrify us out of this city, but we gon' be alright

When you know, we been hurt, been down before, n***a
When my pride was low, lookin' at the world like, where do we go, n***a?
And we hate Popo, wanna kill us dead in the street for sure, n***a
I'm at the preacher's door
My knees gettin' weak and my gun might blow but we gon' be alright

CLOSING PRAYER

Heavenly Father we are living in a time where it is easy to become depressed. It is easy to lose hope and give up. We need You to adjust our perspective and lift our countenance so that we can see life the way that You see it. Thank you for the reassurance that everything is going to be alright. Our community will be alright and most importantly our future will be alright. In Jesus' name I pray, Amen.

CHAPTER 4 - REFLECTION QUESTIONS

1. How can knowing our history assist us in the present struggle for social justice?
2. Why is it empowering to not envy the power or wealth of the wicked?
3. How do we offer hope to our community in the midst of systemic oppression?

CHAPTER 5

The Preacher's Guide to Visiting the White House

David and Nathan's conversation demonstrates to us that God
notices the injustices taking place in this world and that Prophets,
as well as the Church, have a responsibility to speak truth to
power with the hope that man will reconcile with God.

2 Samuel 12:1-15

This past week, we saw how 40 "inner city" (mostly African-
American) pastors met with Donald Trump around the issues
affecting minority communities like Prison Reform, Job Growth, etc.
Many, including the White House, have called the meeting a success.
Pastor Darrell Scott (y'all know him, one of the President's puppet
preachers) said, *"This is probably the most pro-active administration
regarding urban America and the faith-based community in my lifetime...
This is probably going to be ... the most pro-black president that we've had
in our lifetime." "This president actually wants to prove something to our
community, our faith-based community and our ethnic community." "The
last president didn't feel like he had to."*

Now, I'm not going to waste your time trying to unpack all of that
foolishness. However, when you make comments like Trump being
"pro-active regarding urban America" and "Trump possibly being the
most pro-Black president of our lifetime" and "then taking shots at
President Obama," now you're misleading people who probably trust

you as a spiritual leader and may actually believe you have their best interest at heart.

As I learned more about the event, I thought to myself, "How could these preachers allow themselves and the office they hold to be manipulated by a well-documented liar, racist, and possible ally of the Russian government?" This is the same president who's taken photos with Black entertainers and athletes while telling them he would work on their issues. This same president brought a large number of Black college presidents to the White House under the same premise only to use them for a photo-op and now this group of Black preachers are the latest group to be manipulated by our resident Liar-in-Chief.

Brother pastor and sister pastor, how can you go to the White House and not challenge this president on why he refers to African countries as s-hole countries? How can you not challenge him on why Black NFL players who are protesting and standing for the same issues you claim to be advocating for are referred to as SOBs? How can we have prison reform when your own Justice Department is stopping or reversing the Obama Administration investigations into police departments and sheriff offices all over this country? How are we going to have real criminal justice reform when the Justice Department won't investigate Freddie Gray in Baltimore or Tamir Rice in Cleveland or Eric Garner in New York or Sandra Bland in Texas?

In the Bible, has there ever been a time when God sent a prophet to be silent? Whenever a prophet had to confront a leader, they spoke truth to power, realizing that there may be consequences. Elijah knew Ahab did not like him. As a matter of fact, Ahab called him a troublemaker. Daniel confronted Nebuchadnezzar and John the Baptist knew he had to confront Herod and his sin.

It is when preachers act like the ones we saw this week that people begin to lose faith in Christianity, not realizing there is a difference between slave-holder religion and true Christianity. Slaveholder religion began back in slavery times as a way to control the minds of enslaved Africans while dehumanizing them in order to justify enslaving our ancestors. You see, once I take away your humanity, I can treat you any type of way without feeling any kind of moral conviction. Even worse, if you tell me God's cool with it, I won't have any guilt, moral or otherwise, as to how I treat you.

Back then, White preachers said Blacks were cursed, misquoting Genesis 9 with the alleged curse of Ham. When in reality, God cursed Canaan. Then misinterpreting Paul in Ephesians 6 when he said, "slaves obey your masters." Understand that slavery in this country was justified not just politically, not just legally, but also religiously.

This is why our sisters and brothers who don't share our melanin can call themselves Christians and act racist at the same time. This same religion today still has our people wandering through the wilderness of oppression with hopes of getting to the promised land of freedom, justice and equality.

I'm not against White preachers, because obviously Black ones can mislead you just as fast. You and I need good preaching and a Christianity that speaks to both who we are and Whose we are. Our ancestors understood this religion when they chose to ignore the slaveholder religion and focus more on the narrative in Exodus and saw Jesus as one who they could relate to, being wrongly convicted and lynched. Our ancestors embraced the prophets of the Old Testament who spoke truth to power—like **Amos 5:24** when he said, "*Let justice roll down like waters and righteousness like a mighty stream*" and **Micah 6:8** who said, "*What does the Lord require but to do justice love mercy and walk humbly with our God,*" Our ancestors embraced <u>Jesus'</u> message, when He quoted <u>Isaiah 61</u> in **Luke 4:18-19:**

"The Spirit of the Lord is upon Me,
Because He has anointed Me
To preach the gospel to the poor;
He has sent Me to heal the brokenhearted,
To proclaim liberty to the captives
And recovery of sight to the blind,
To set at liberty those who are oppressed;
To proclaim the acceptable year of the Lord."

That's why Jesus said in **Luke 10:27,** "*Love the Lord your God with all your heart and with all your soul and with all your strength and* *with all your mind.*" You're supposed to bring your mind to church. So many of us have been trained to use church as a form of escape from the world, for me to stand up here for 30 minutes and tell you "Won't He do it," or "Your breakthrough's on the way," not realizing that the church is not where you go to get away from your problems, but to know how to navigate a world filled with hate, racism and greed in a way that pushes God's Kingdom and gives Him glory.

You see, you don't need me to tell you the story about Daniel in the Lions' Den or how Moses parted the Red Sea. You don't need me to tell you about Jesus raising Lazarus from the dead. No, you can read those stories on your own. You come to church to get wisdom and insight— wisdom and insight as to how to handle and live in this world – so that we can go out into the world and make a difference.

This is the season for the church to get back to being the church; for prophets and men and women of God to start speaking truth to power, calling out evil when you see it, and making your presence felt in the community.

People of God, we are living in a time where it looks like we can't catch a break. Since November 9, 2016, there has been this feeling that the country is moving backwards and not forward. Every day, it feels like there's new legislation or an executive order designed to continue to keep Black and Brown people on the fringes of society.

I need somebody to know today that when it seems **bleak**, God is at His **best**. We may be down, but we're not out. "*We are hard-pressed on every side, yet not crushed; we are perplexed, but not in despair; persecuted, but not forsaken; struck down, but not destroyed.*" We serve a God who promised to never leave us nor forsake us!

I like to give people the benefit of the doubt. So, through scripture, I want to help these pastors and those who may go to the White House in the future, how you should conduct yourself when speaking on behalf of vulnerable people.

In today's text, we see the man of God (the prophet Nathan) being used by God to confront and chastise the governmental power structure of the day, being represented by King David about the injustice that he carried out and then tried to cover up. The text reminds us today that

God sees all things and that His judgment and justice will have the final say.

Let me give you the context to help you better appreciate the content.

You all know the story. When you get a chance, go back and read chapter 11. But lest I hold you too long today, let me give you the cliff notes version. David should have been off to war with his men but he was at home walking on the roof. Let me parenthetically pause for a moment. When you're in the wrong place, it's only a matter of time before you end up doing the wrong thing. Somebody knows what I'm talking about. If everybody's smoking a joint, it's only a matter of time before it comes around to you. When you're not in the ministry God called you to, it's only a matter of time before you mess up the ministry you're in. If you don't go where God tells you to go, it's only a matter of time before you've wasted years of your life and the years of whoever else is around you.

So, David is walking on the roof and he sees this "hotty with a body" by the name of Bathsheba. She's naked from having bathed, which was the custom during that day, and David just had to have her. David got in his feelings like Drake and asked Bathsheba, *"Do you love me? Are you riding? Say you'll never ever leave from beside me, 'Cause I want you and I need you, And I'm down for you always."* **That may be too millennial.** David said, *"She's a brick house, the lady's stacked and that's a fact, ain't holding nothing back!"*

So, he sends someone to find out about her. He finds out she's married to Uriah and that she's the daughter of one of his warriors, Eliam. Even after knowing she's married, he sends for her and sleeps with her.

I don't know why y'all watch Empire, Greenleaf and The Haves and The Have Nots, or Love and Hip-Hop. If you would just get in this Bible, you will have all the drama you need!

So, David sleeps with Bathsheba and gets her pregnant. Now David is trying to figure out how to cover this up. How many of you have heard the saying, "Once you find yourself in a hole, stop digging?" Next, David sends for Uriah, who is in the right place, on the battlefield and tries to buddy up to him. After he and Uriah hangout, David sends him home so that Uriah would sleep with his wife Bathsheba and David could cover up this whole pregnancy. But Uriah refuses to even go into his house, because he was an honorable man and refused to lay with his wife until he came back from war. You would think that the level of integrity that Uriah is showing would wake up something in David to do the right thing.

The next night, David throws a party and the palace is turnt up. He gets Uriah drunk and says, *"Ok Uriah, go home, I know Bathsheba is missing you, go handle your business player."* David sends him home and he wakes up the next day to find out that Uriah is sleeping at the entrance of the palace with David's servants. Now David realizes that he has a problem.

So, he sends Uriah back out to war, this time with a note for his commanding officer, Joab, to put Uriah on the frontlines, guaranteeing that he gets killed in battle. So, in essence, you have an executive order written by one branch of government to carry out the extermination of a man by another agency of government. Now the murder and cover up of Uriah has now become State sanctioned and systemic. We now have the entire system working against a man who lacks privilege, power and status to protect neither himself nor his family. He is now at the mercy of a government he gave his life to serve. Look at somebody and ask, does this sound familiar?

So, Uriah is killed in battle, David marries Bathsheba and she gives birth to him a son and it looks like this whole episode is over. But the absolute last sentence of **Chapter 11** simply reads, *"**But the thing that David had done displeased the Lord.**"* Be careful when you're out here doing dirt. People might not see you but God sees everything!

So, Nathan, the prophet, is called by God to confront David about his sin. We are first introduced to Nathan in chapter 7, where Nathan is telling David the promises of God.

That's how it is for a lot of clergy. We initially meet people in power during happy times—the inauguration, the swearing in, a prayer breakfast, etc. But if we are true to our calling, there are going to be times when we have to speak truth to power. Dr. King once said, *"**The** *church must be reminded that it is not the master or the servant of the state. It must be the guide and critic of the state, and never its tool."*

Here, Nathan has to pay a different type of visit to the palace. When speaking truth to power, you have to still frame your speech carefully. So, instead of coming out guns blazing, Nathan looks to soften the blow with a parable before announcing the judgment of the Lord. So, Nathan begins with the parable of the rich man and the poor man, stressing the point that the poor man had nothing but this one baby lamb. Nathan spoke of how this lamb was a part of the poor man's family, how it grew up with his daughter, and in contrast, how this rich man had flocks of lambs.

We can see how Uriah has only one wife while David has wives and concubines. But then this "traveler" comes along—this traveler could be seen as David's own lust, and instead of feeding this lust with his own flock, he takes all that the other man has.

In other words, David uses his power and authority to prey on the weak. So, in keeping with the story, in order to show hospitality to the traveler, the rich man takes from the poor man and neither the rich man nor the traveler see anything wrong with this picture. There's no sense of injustice. The feeling is your status negates your voice. Why should I spend some of my millions when I can just take some of yours? It's easier for me to steal your land, steal your labor and essentially and eventually steal your life!

David is shocked and angry at this arbitrary taking and says in **verses 5 & 6, "As the Lord lives, the man who has done this shall surely die! And he shall restore fourfold for the lamb, because he did this thing and because he had no pity."** That word 'pity' is closer to the word 'compassion,' especially the compassion that saves from death. In other words, the rich man lacked the compassion to save the life of that lamb from the slaughter. Much like David lacked the compassion to spare Uriah's life.

Isn't that what we expect from those in power, compassion? How can you be in power and lack the compassion to supply healthcare to millions? How can you be in power and have no compassion for the poor? How can you be in power and have no compassion for an unarmed Black person being shot and killed? David hit it right on the head when he declared the man should die and repay and restore what he owes fourfold!

Suddenly, Nathan hits him with the Floyd Mayweather knockout blow in verse 7, *"David you are the man!"* Nathan reveals to David "I'm talking about you!" He further tells David that he is the strong taking advantage of the weak; he is the privileged exploiting the poor; he is the powerful crushing the powerless—David you are the man!

David had become that which he despised. Every now and then, you and I need to self-evaluate our moves and our motives to make sure we don't allow power to intoxicate us or insulate us from showing love and compassion to our fellow sisters and brothers.

Nathan then begins to tell David all that God did for him up to this point, all that God had given to him—and that God would have given him more! But David has not just sinned against Uriah and Bathsheba, but he has sinned against God Himself and that has brought the judgment of God on his house. All of the terror and violence that will come upon David's kingdom and home, from his son dying to another son, Absalom, rising up against him, all because of his sin.

People of God, the fact is this, there will be justice for Uriah. Though he's dead, just like when Cain killed Abel, his blood will cry out from the ground. It looked like the system won; it looked like the cover up was successful; it looked like the legislation would accomplish its goal—but God is a God of justice.

Though Philando Castile is dead, there will still be justice for him. There will still be justice for Trayvon Martin, Tamir Rice, Rekia Boyd, Alton Sterling and Mike Brown. Momma and Grand Momma used to say, "He may not come when you want Him, but He's always right on time!" God's timing is always right!

Sisters and brothers, we are in the season where God is raising up Nathans to speak His truth to power. There are too many folks in power that think they can get away with anything and we know where they get it. The current president once said during the last campaign, *"I could stand in the middle of 5th Avenue and shoot somebody and I wouldn't lose any votes."* That may be true Mr. Trump, but there's a lot more you can lose than votes. Jesus said, **"What does it profit a man to gain the whole world and lose his soul?"** <u>Proverbs 10:27</u>: *"The fear of the LORD adds* *length to life, but the years of the wicked are cut short."* <u>Psalm 37:1, 2</u>: *"Fret not thyself because of evildoers, neither be thou envious against the workers of iniquity. For they shall soon be cut down like the grass, and wither as the green herb."*

Sisters and brothers, what I love about this story is not just the pronouncement of God's judgment, but also a call for reconciliation. Once David is told of his sin, he immediately repents in **verse 13**. He says, *"I have sinned against the Lord."* David doesn't reject Nathan; his heart turns toward repentance. It is that revelation that causes David to later write **Psalm 51**, *"Create in me a clean heart, O God, And renew a steadfast spirit within me. Do not cast me away from Your presence, and do not take Your Holy Spirit from me."*

That's the second part of our calling. Not only are we called to speak truth to power, but to forge a path toward confession and reconciliation by showing the sinner that he's wrong and to bring him or her back to God. The Bible says, *"If my people, which are called by my name, shall humble themselves, and pray, and seek my face, and turn from their wicked ways; then will I hear from heaven, and will forgive their sin, and will heal their land."*[6]

To "turn" in the Hebrew means, "to repent or go in the other direction." When I speak truth to power, I'm trying to turn our society, our world and my enemy in another direction. I don't just want to condemn, I want to convert. I don't want to just chastise, I want to see change. I don't want to just protest, I want to see progress. I'm not looking just to confront, but I want to find common ground.

We serve a God who knows what it's like to be exploited by the system. He knows what it's like to be taken advantage of in the courts. He is a Savior who knows what it's like to have the system against you; a Savior who knows about being a refugee and having to flee your country, because your life is in danger.

Verse 15 says, *"[Then] Nathan went to his house.""* The prophet went to the palace and did what God wanted him to do, said what God wanted him to say, and then went home. The calling is to speak truth to power, and then go back home. He didn't try to become David's boy.

---

[6] 2 Chronicles 7:14, *Holy Bible*

He didn't become David's golf buddy. He didn't go out and speak the administration's talking points. He didn't go there for a photo-op.

Nathan was able to go back home with integrity, authority and with the respect of his people. He went back to his house, his calling; the vineyard God called him to.

Always keep your integrity. Don't give in to the pressures of this world for popularity or fame at the expense of your calling and the ministry God has called you to.

CLOSING PRAYER

Most wise and holy God, it is with a bowed head and humble spirit in which I come to you. Please touch our leaders so that when they are in spaces of power that there must be an unadulterated "Thus saith the Lord" on their lips. Also, God help me to keep this in mind when you position me to be a voice for the voiceless. In Jesus name I pray. Amen

CHAPTER 5 - REFLECTION QUESTIONS

1. Why is it important for the people of God to speak truth to power?
2. What lessons can we take away from David and Nathan? The African-American Pastors and President Trump?
3. How can we ensure that we don't find ourselves being used by the powers that be when we should be speaking and standing on behalf of the people of God?

CHAPTER 6

"God's Plan"

While the wicked are winning, my past perspective informs me that
God's plan is not subject to my circumstances. God will be faithful
in my future, while guiding my every step through this season.

Psalm 37:23-26

Saints, a few years ago I remember watching a movie called 12 Years
A Slave. How many of you remember that movie? The movie is based
upon the real-life account of Solomon Northrop, an educated and free
Black man living in New York during the time of slavery.

Solomon Northrop is convinced to go to Washington, DC by two
White men for short-term employment for playing the violin. One night,
he's out drinking with the two White men and they drug him so that he
passes out. The next morning, Solomon wakes up in the South in chains.
Not realizing, until later in the film, that they had kidnapped him and
sold him into slavery. The movie chronicles how for 12 years and various
plantations, Solomon, who's been given the name Platt, has to continue
to try to keep his dignity, hope against hope, and believe that he would
be returned back to his family and former life again.

Have you ever been in a situation where it looked like you couldn't
get out? Where you didn't have the strength or the resources to get out?
Where even the people around you told you this is how it's always going
to be?

Fast forward, Solomon ends up getting released when he hears the plantation master and a White guy from Canada, named Samuel Bass, arguing about the inhumanity of American slavery. So, Solomon convinces Samuel Bass to mail a letter he's written to a friend of his, Mr. Parker, a White shopkeeper in New York. Shortly thereafter, the Sheriff arrives on the plantation with Mr. Parker and Solomon is released.

There is a powerful quote in the movie where Solomon is sitting and talking with some other enslaved Africans. One of them tells Solomon that in order to survive around here, you need to keep your head, stop talking about being free and don't tell anybody who you are. You need to try to survive. <u>Solomon responds by saying</u>, *"Days ago, I was with my family, in my home. Now you're telling me all that's lost? Tell no one who I am, that's the way to survive? Well, I don't want to survive. I want to live."*

Is that your testimony today? I don't just want to survive, I want to live. God didn't put me here to pay bills, struggle and die; no, I want to live. I know that I'm gifted and I refuse to pretend like all I can do is my job and manage my home; no I want to live. I thank God for my children and my grandchildren, but God didn't put me here just to raise them and give them money; no I want to live!

People of God, life has a way of making you feel like Solomon Northrop. One day your life is going fine, you and your family are making it and your career is taking off and then literally overnight you can wake up to a nightmare. One day you're feeling good in your body, then the doctor calls with your test results. You wake up one day and your child is doing well and later you get a call that they've been arrested. Life has a way (as the old folks would say) of turning on a dime.

But there is Good News today! God, through His Word, is actively telling you and me that we can trust that He's with us and guiding us even when it looks like all hell is breaking loose around us. God's plan and His presence are not subject to the conditions of our lives. He's the same God on the mountaintop as He is in the valley. As a matter of fact, the Lord draws nearer to us in difficult times. **Psalm 34:18:** *"The Lord is near to the brokenhearted and saves the crushed in spirit."*

We serve a God that does not change; a God whose presence we never have to doubt. We serve a God whose character we never have to question. **Hebrews 13:8:** *"Christ is the same yesterday, today and forever!"* In today's text, David reassures us that through it all, God has a plan.

Let me give you the context to help you better appreciate the content.

David, in his old age, is reminding the believer that while the wicked are winning, the righteous can still make progress with the Lord's help. Not only that, but God has set and established the moves we should make during this season. God is pleased with us even though the journey is difficult.

David never said it would be easy, but he reassured the reader that God will never forsake, abandon or leave behind those who are righteous. Also, the seed of the righteous will have their needs met.

David, here in these three short verses, is looking back over his life. He's looking at all of the changes and challenges, all of the obstacles he's had to overcome and all of the detours and disappointments that have brought him to this place.

David was ruminating and reminiscing in the tone and tenor of the old church hymn:

As I look back over my life
And I think things over I can truly say that I've been blessed
I've got a testimony!

When is the last time you looked back over your life and realized that God's hand has been all over your *entire* life? Not just your saved life; not since you've learned how to pray; not since you stopped going to the club; not since you've learned how to quote scripture—but I'm talking about realizing that God—through His providence and protection, His foresight and His farsightedness, has been guiding you every step of the way.

"The steps of a man are established by the Lord, when he delights in his way;

though he fall, he shall not be cast headlong, for the Lord upholds his hand."

How many of you know that in the midst of this season, God is ordering your steps? Yes, the enemy is winning while the righteous are wanting; yes, racism is everywhere. As a matter of fact, they're having a "Unite the Right" rally today, not too far from here. They think they are putting a plan in place while God is really preparing their downfall.

It's hard for many of us to understand that our steps, every move we make is established or "ordered" (KJV) by the Lord. That word, "established (or ordered)," in Hebrew means, "to set, establish or prepare." **In other words, God has laid out how you are to move in the midst of this season**. He's inspected the terrain and has put the right people in your path to help you along the way.

God is so bad (Ebonics for good) that He doesn't have to change your situation, but He can show you how to walk through it. **Isaiah 43:2: "When you pass through the waters, I will be with you; and through the rivers, they shall not overwhelm you; when you walk through fire you shall not be burned, and the flame shall not consume you."**

I remember going through a difficult season of my life and being on the phone with a preacher friend of mine and him saying, *"Spann, you are going to have to know what God's voice sounds like for yourself."* In other words, this situation is not going to change and a whole lot of people are going to be in your ear, but you're going to have to figure out what to do next. You have to make sure that you're walking in the steps that God has already ordered and established.

Sometimes in life when we get into difficult and debilitating situations, our immediate cry is for God to get us out and sometimes He does. But many times, we don't need deliverance, we just need to know what the next step is.

Every now and then, our prayer needs to be "Lord, what do I do next; what's the next step; what should I pray for? Lord, how do you want to use me in this season?" Then in the same verse, the Bible says, "God delights in his way." That word, "delight," means, "to incline, to be pleased with or well-pleased." You want to please God in this season, you want Him to incline to you—then trust Him to show you the next step!

49

Now this is not easy. How do you know Spann? **Verse 24:** *"though he fall, he shall not be cast headlong, for the Lord upholds his hand.* (NKJV) *Though he fall, he will not be utterly cast down."* In other words, it's going to be difficult; you and I are going to make mistakes; there will be times when the enemy gets the best of us. There will be times when we will be standing in the midst of a mess and it will be all our fault.

But we will not be cast headlong or utterly cast down. God's not going to throw us away. That will not be the end of our story. Our lives will not end with our errors nor will the wicked have the last word. As a matter of fact, the second part of **verse 24** says, *"For the Lord upholds his hand."* In other words, like a referee in a boxing match or in the mixed martial arts—you see 2 men (or women) standing next to each other and both of them look beat up, eyes all swollen, cuts on their face, blood everywhere—then the referee grabs one of them by the hand and raises it!

That's what God will do for you and for me. We're going to go through difficult times; times of sickness; times of mourning loved ones; times of losing a job or losing a home; times when I want to give up and even times of church hurt. However, this Bible that we believe, this chapter that we've chosen and this verse that we're viewing says that in the end—though I'm tired, though I'm worn and though it looks like I should lose—the Lord will uphold my hand in victory!

People of God, while the wicked are winning, my past perspective should inform me that God's plan is not subject to my *circumstances.* God will be faithful in my future while guiding my every step through this season.

Drake has a song called, *God's Plan,* where he talks about all of the attacks that have come against him and how his enemies have wanted to see him fall. In the chorus, he says, *"Bad things, It's a lot of bad things That they wishin' and wishin' and wishin' and wishin' They wishin' on me."* I need you to know today that your enemies are wishing to see you fall; wishing to see you give up; wishing to see you throw in the towel.

But God! They can wish, but they can't stop God's will. They can plot, but they can't stop God's plan. They can try, but my God is triumphant. This week, I want you to pray for the next step God wants you to take. Don't get caught up in trying to fix everything, just remind God that He promised to order your steps and guide your path.

David makes some bold claims in this text. He claimed that God will guide our steps, be delighted and incline unto us, and that God will declare us the victor! David should be a motivational speaker like Willie Jolley, Les Brown or somebody, because verses 23-24 are very inspiring. My question for David would be, "How can you be so sure? David, how can you speak so matter of fact about God? David, how can you be so sure that God is empowering His people while the wicked are winning?"

Verse 25-26 (and I'm done) *I have been young, and now am old, yet I have not seen the righteous forsaken or his children begging for bread. He is ever lending generously, and his children become a blessing.*

David said I know God will order your steps; I know He'll delight in your way; I know God will uphold your hand, because I've seen Him do it! I've seen Him help me defeat Goliath. God was with me when Saul was trying to kill me and I was hiding in caves. God still loved me even after what I did to Bathsheba and Uriah—*I was young but now I'm old...*

Is there anybody here that has lived long enough to know that God will work it out? Every now and then you need to remind yourself that I don't have these gray hairs for nothing. I might walk a little slower, but I know God is faithful. I might not remember like I used to, but I know God will bring me out! *I was young but now I'm old...*

David said that he has never seen the righteous forsaken. That word, "forsaken," means "abandoned, to leave behind, to leave in a lurch or to leave someone who is depending on your services."

I don't know who I'm talking to, but God won't let you down:

He promised— to never leave you nor forsake you
He promised—no weapon formed against you shall prosper
He promised—weeping may endure for a night, but joy will come in the morning
He promised—all things work together for the good of those who love the Lord

I have been young, and now am old, yet I have not seen the righteous forsaken

He sealed His promise in blood:
On a hill far away, stood an old rugged Cross
The emblem of suffering and shame
And I love that old Cross where the dearest and best
For a world of lost sinners was slain
So I'll cherish the old rugged Cross
Till my trophies at last I lay down
I will cling to the old rugged Cross
And exchange it some day for a crown

I have been young, and now am old, yet I have not seen the righteous forsaken or his children begging for bread. He is ever lending generously, and his children become a blessing.

<u>There are generational blessings attached to how you walk through this season.</u> We must believe that our faithfulness during this season will be a blessing to and for the generation that will follow us. It is all a part of God's Plan.

CLOSING PRAYER

Gracious and mighty God, I thank you for having a plan for my life and for all of your people. It is during the difficult times when it looks like injustice is winning and those of us who believe in you feel powerless. Help us during the dark days to know that the sun of justice and peace and equality will indeed shine again. Grant us patience through the process of speaking truth to power and fighting for a better society. In Jesus name I pray, Amen.

CHAPTER 6 - REFLECTION QUESTIONS

1. Why is it difficult for us to remember that God has already ordered every step we take in life?
2. In the struggle for justice, why is it important to keep reminding both ourselves and those who fight with us that God's plan will eventually prevail?
3. Discuss the importance of having a movement that embraces people of all ages (see verses 25-26)?

CHAPTER 7

"What Justice Looks Like"

God is reminding the saints to always be steadfast, immovable,
always abounding in the Lord. Those of us who embrace
the social justice aspects of the Gospel are fighting the
good fight and we are on the right side of history. Most
importantly, our time of vindication will come quickly.

Psalm 37:28

People of God, I'd like to tell you a story about a man by the name of
Jarrett Adams. Mr. Adams was recently featured on NBC News with
Lester Holt. **Jarrett Adams, at age 17, had just finished high school on
the South Side of Chicago when he decided to go to a party with some
of his friends on the campus of the University of Wisconsin**. After
having what Adams called a consensual encounter with a woman there,
three weeks later he is preparing to enter junior college, when he was
arrested for sexual assault.

Being a young Black man and having no experience with the
criminal justice system, he relied solely on the advice of his lawyer. **Now,
understand that Jarrett is innocent of this crime**. Jarrett denied the
crime from the beginning and just knew that this would be cleared up
shortly. So, the attorney says "Hey, they (the State) hasn't proven its case,
so you have nothing to worry about—the best defense is no defense. So,
his attorney doesn't investigate, doesn't put on any witnesses and then
sits Jarrett, this 17-year-old Black teen in front of an all-White jury. Now

y'all know what happened next. Jarred gets convicted and sentenced to 28 years in prison.

While Jarrett is in prison, his cellmate, who works in the prison law library, says to him:

> "Listen. I go over hundreds of inmates' cases, and all of them say the same thing: 'I'm innocent.' He said, 'I've never seen a case like yours before. You're in here for some racist bull crap, and you've essentially waved the white flag.'"

Then his cellmate (watch this) urged him not to give up:

> "It's only going to take a second before you have tattoos on your face and have given up and completely don't care at all. You need to go down swinging."

Is there anybody here who has found himself or herself in a situation like Jarrett? You're thinking, "This is bad, but it will get cleared up quickly?" You see, your life is going off track and you feel like there's nothing you can do about it? They fire you from your job, the doctor calls to discuss your blood work, unexpected bill after unexpected bill, folks begin to scandalize your name; you find out your Boo don't want you or you realize your Bae don't want to stay—like the commercial says, "life comes at you fast."

Not only is your situation so suffocating, but you feel your faith fleeing and your heart is heavy, and you want to give up and throw in the towel. But then something or someone reminds you, like Jarrett Adams' cellmate, *"I've got to go down swinging?"*

Yes, I'm down, but I'm not out. Yes, it looks bleak, but I'm still blessed. I'm hurting, but I can still be healed. People may leave me, but God still loves me. *"I've got to go down swinging!"* **Tell your neighbor, "Go down swinging!"**

I just can't give up now, I've come too far from where I started from— The more you talk about me, the more I'll testify; the more you lie, the more I'll lift up my eyes to the hills; the more you plot, the more I'll pray; the more you try to frame me, the more I'll fast. We don't fight the way the world fights. **2 Corinthians 10:4** says, *"For the weapons of our warfare are not carnal, but mighty through God to the pulling down of strong holds."*

Don't ever allow the enemy to intimidate you with money, job security, physical violence, or even police intervention. You see, they have their weapons and we have ours. The Bible says that they locked up Paul and Silas, but at midnight they were praying and singing hymns. Even the walls of Jericho fell when the people shouted. The Lord told King Hezekiah that he was going to die, but Hezekiah prayed and the Lord added 15 years to his life!

When the enemy comes for you, you've got to remind yourself that I have some weapons at my disposal. I may not have a gun, but I have goodness and mercy following me. I may not have finances, but I have a Friend who sticks closer than a brother. The courts might be against me, but I have Christ the solid rock I stand all other ground is sinking sand!

In today's text, David reminds us that we serve a God of justice. Not just a God who likes justice, but who loves justice.

Let me give you the context to help you better appreciate the content.

As we know by now, David, in his old age, is emphatically telling the reader that God, Who is Master and Lord of all, especially the people of Israel, deeply cares about and has His heart knit to the righteous receiving justice. God will not cast off or abandon the righteous, which means that although it may not come swiftly, the righteous will receive justice.

Here, this text forces us to deal with the evangelical community. Evangelicals want you to believe that all God cares about is soul winning, gay marriage and abortion. The rest of this stuff is not important. Never mind Jesus talking about preaching the Gospel to the poor and setting at liberty those who are oppressed or Moses freeing his people from slavery. It's like the Wizard of Oz, after he got exposed; he said, "Don't pay attention to the man behind the curtain!"

I always remind everyone to stop listening to preachers who are giving you 21st century slave religion. All slave religion does is misinterpret the Bible with the expressed intent to make you mentally and spiritually impotent, therefore, separating you from the true Christ-intended emancipation for yourself and your community.

Everybody wants to tell you how God is going to bless you and take you to the next level and to not worry about these social issues. But the Bible says that God is concerned about these issues. Maybe I can't get to the next level, because I'm unable to get an adequate education. Maybe I can't get to the next level, because of a school-to-prison pipeline, where they look at the test scores of elementary school children to determine how many prisons to build. Maybe I can't get to the next level, because joblessness and income inequality plague my community and keeps me and people who look like me in repeated cycles of poverty. Jesus said in **John 8:32,** *"And you will know the truth and the truth will set you free."* If what you're hearing doesn't set you free, then it isn't the truth!

Verse 28 says, *"For the Lord loves justice; he will not forsake his saints. They are preserved forever, but the children of the wicked shall be cut off."* The Lord loves justice. That word, "love," here in Hebrew is translated as "a deep affection, an affinity towards or to be deeply attached to. God doesn't just like justice or just think it's a good idea, nor is He indifferent toward justice. This Bible that we believe, this chapter that we've chosen and this verse that we're viewing, says, "The Lord <u>loves</u> justice!" If God loves justice, it must be important to Him.

Think about what you love in life, i.e. your spouse, your children, family and friends. Now think about what you would do to protect what you love! God loves justice! The word, "justice" (the KJV uses the word 'judgment'), in this instance, can be broken down into two parts. The first part is a judge presiding over a case and rendering the proper verdict, while the second part protects the rights of the participants.

In his book, *The Little Book of Biblical Justice,* Chris Marshall gives us a great biblical definition of justice. He quotes, "...justice entails the exercise of legitimate power to ensure that benefits and penalties are distributed fairly and equitable in society, thus meeting the rights and enforcing the obligations of all parties."[7]

The second part of verse 28 says, *"He will not forsake his saints. They are preserved forever, but the children of the wicked shall be cut*

---

[7] Marshall, Chris, *The Little Book of Biblical Justice* (Good Books 2005); Page 7

off." What this lets us know is that justice doesn't always come when we want it. There may be times when you feel neglected. It feels like every day there's a new police shooting video being released. Every day, 45, tweets something to upset most of America. I recently saw how priests in Pennsylvania were able to molest over a thousand children for many, many years. I say all of this to say that sometimes the reign of the unrighteous and the era of evil extends longer than we think it should, but thanks be to God that He doesn't forget— ***but the children of the wicked shall be cut off.*** In other words, if this goes to the next generation, God will make sure that justice is granted on behalf of His children.

God is reminding the saints to always be steadfast, immovable always abounding in the Lord. Those of us who embrace the social justice aspects of the Gospel are fighting the good fight and we are on the right side of history. Most importantly, our time of vindication will come quickly.

Dr. Cornel West once said, *"Justice is what love looks like in public."* Remember, God is love. If we truly loved one another, we wouldn't, and we couldn't, look the other way when a sister or brother is done wrong. If we loved each other, we wouldn't let police officers go free after killing unarmed Black people. If we truly loved each other, we wouldn't separate families at the border and put children in cages. If we really loved each other, we would pay a living wage to workers so that people can keep a roof over their heads and feed their children with dignity.

We cannot claim to be a Christian nation if we do not love that which God loves, and that is justice.

As I take my seat, I guess I should tell you how Mr. Jarrett Adams' case worked out. If you remember, Jarrett was arrested and given a 28-year prison sentence at the age of 17. After taking the advice of his cellmate, Jarrett decided to fight the case. So, Jarrett started reading law books and he finds a Supreme Court decision that worked in his favor. So, Jarrett called the Innocence Project, which is an organization that works to get decisions overturned for people who have been wrongly convicted.

Jarrett convinced the lawyer at the Innocence Project to use his argument. His case gets overturned and the charges get dropped. The story gets better. A month after Jarrett is freed in 2007, he enrolls in Community College, goes on to get a Bachelor's Degree and eventually gets a law degree. Then last summer, he became the first Innocence Project exoneree to be hired as an attorney by the organization.

I need somebody to know today, that Jarrett's story is exactly what justice looks like. It looks like a man wrongly convicted, the system has failed him and a feeling like there's no way out. But God, being a lover of justice, steps in and declares, "Overturned!" He may not come when you want Him but He's always right on time!

Has God ever overturned some stuff in your life?

- The doctor gave you 6 months to live, but God said, "Overturned!"
- The court thought they were going to lock you up, but God said, "Overturned!"
- The school gave up on your child, but God said, "Overturned!'
- Your family told you you'd never be anything, but God said, "Overturned!"
- You thought you couldn't come back from being fired, but God said, "Overturned!"
- You thought you'd never be happy again but God said. "Overturned!

The Bible says:

- **Abraham and Sarah** didn't think they could have children, but God said, "Overturned."
- **Joseph's brothers** threw him in a pit and sold him into slavery, but God said, "Overturned."
- They put **Daniel** in a lions' den, but the king woke up the next morning and saw God said, "Overturned."
- **Queen Esther** said, "If I perish, let me perish," but God said, "Overturned."
- There was a man named, **Jesus.** They hung Him high and stretched Him wide. He hung His head, for you and me He died. But early Sunday morning God declared Overturned and He rose with all power in heaven and earth in His hands!

There are some things that are going to be overturned in your life. Ask God to look at your case again. Ask God to look at your dream again. Ask God for a second opinion on your doctor's report. Ask God to reevaluate your job status. I believe God is going to overturn some previous decisions. God is going to reopen your case. He's going to have a change of heart. He's going to see your situation covered under the blood of Jesus! Watch what God will do when you ask Him to overturn your case!

CLOSING PRAYER

Dear God, thank you for telling us in your Word that You love justice. Help us as a society to love justice just as much as You do. Help us to fight for justice every day. Most importantly, remind us that You are fighting right alongside of us. In Jesus' name, I pray, Amen.

CHAPTER 7 - REFLECTION QUESTIONS

1. Why is it important to know that God loves justice?
2. Specifically, what should justice look like in your community? What should justice look like in America?
3. How can we get more of those who are in the body of Christ to love justice as God states in His Word?

CHAPTER 8

"Until My Change Comes"

God is reassuring us that our waiting and trusting in Him
will not be in vain. Though the exploits of the wicked make it
difficult, it is our godly discipline together with trusting God's
Word that will guarantee God's deliverance and protection.

Psalm 37:34-40

The late, great Dr. Gardner C. Taylor, pastor emeritus of the Concord
Baptist Church in Brooklyn, NY, known by many as the "Dean of
American Preaching," once said about patience:

> *"Patience does not work in a vacuum. It does not function
> in a life that is not turned toward God. God's promises
> are open to every person. Don't be anxious. Because of
> your faith, you can trust in the goodness of God above.
> In that trust, anxiety vanishes; care flees as clouds before
> the sunshine.*
>
> *"What a great sense of freedom we have in turning
> over all of our cares and concerns to God. This is the
> person who says, "I will take all God wants me to have
> and I will be calm when God holds back from me." We
> have a peace that as we travel the seas of life, we have the
> greatest captain who ever sailed."*

That's Good News today! I can be calm, because God is the captain of the ship. I can have peace, because God is my pilot. I can go on and take a nap, because God is navigating the direction of my life! Every now and then, it's good to know that I can trust the direction of my life, because I have a personal relationship with the Director. He promised to always be with me. The songwriter once said:

> *I've seen the lightning flashing,*
> *And heard the thunder roll,*
> *I've felt sin's breakers dashing,*
> *Trying to conquer my soul;*
> *I've heard the voice of my Savior,*
> *Telling me still to fight on,*
> *He promised never to leave me,*
> *Never to leave me alone.*

Oh, how many of you know that it's hard to get to that level of trust and peace of mind? Truth be told, waiting on God can literally get on your last nerve! How many of you know what it's like to pray to God day after day only to feel like things are getting worse? I wonder who knows what it feels like to know God told you He'd heal your body and you're still sick? Who knows what it's like to be in ministry and waiting for God to move?

In today's world, it's difficult to hear the word, "wait," when we can look out and see the greed of developers in this city move generations of lifelong Black citizens out. Or even worse, the city allowing public housing to fall into disrepair just to justify tearing it down and moving citizens out.

It's difficult to wait and watch another school year begin, while knowing that every child does not have equal access to a quality education; knowing that every individual doesn't have equal access to healthcare. It's hard to hear the word, "wait," while private prisons are profiting off of the pain of Black and Brown communities trapped in this system of mass incarnation, described in detail by Michelle Alexander in her book, *"The New Jim Crow."*[8]

I honestly believe that Dr. Gardner Taylor was on to something

---

[8] Alexander, Michelle, *The New Jim Crow,* (The New Press 2012).

when he said, "*What a great sense of freedom we have in turning over all of our cares and concerns to God.*" Fear is a form of bondage, anxiety is a form of bondage and stress is a form of bondage—**Galatians 5:1, "For freedom Christ has set us free; stand firm therefore, and do not submit again to a yoke of slavery."** People of God, I believe God wants us to be free once and for all. He wants us free from the feelings of powerlessness and pain, as we watch the wicked prosper. He wants us free from anxiety, as to what will happen when our finances are low; free from the stress of what they're doing to us on our jobs.

My sisters and brothers, David, in the closing verses of this Psalm is telling us that the wicked may win the battle, but they won't win the war. Your present difficulty won't destroy you, nor will your current calamity consume you. As a matter of fact, the schemes of the wicked will eventually be shut down.

The text teaches us that we have the aptitude and the ability, the charge and the calling, and the patience and the power to wait until our change comes.

Let me give you the context to help you better appreciate the content.

David is telling the reader to focus intently upon God during this season of watching the wicked rule. God will handle the wicked. It is difficult to keep our focus on God, because everything the wicked is doing is right in our face and they are even flaunting it. God will cut them off. David is also telling us that we will endure attacks, but God will help and deliver us. He is our personal God who will do whatever it takes to keep us from the hand of the enemy.

David reminds us of the importance of waiting on the Lord. **Verse 34 says, "*Wait for the Lord and keep His way, and He will exalt you to inherit the land; you will look on when the wicked are cut off.*"**

First of all, we need to *wait* on the Lord. The word, "wait," here in Hebrew, means "to strain the mind in a certain direction with an expectant attitude or a forward look with assurance." In other words, we are to stretch or pull our minds in the direction of God. Now this isn't easy, because all of my problems are around me. When I wake up,

I feel pain in my body. When I want to buy gas or get some food, I have to make sure I have enough money in my account. My children act as if everything I have told them has gone in one ear and out the other. And don't let me turn the television on and watch story after story of priests in the Catholic church molesting children, watching people lose their homes because of wild fires or daily reliving the trauma of watching violent acts of racism and micro-aggressions against Black and Brown people by the police or other White citizens.

This is why we must be deliberate in turning our focus toward God. This is why horses wear blinders, so that they cannot look to the left or the right, because they would be immediately distracted and take off. This is exactly what God doesn't want us to do. He doesn't want us looking all over the place; He doesn't want us to move suddenly or get startled or make a wrong decision. This is why I must be intentional about keeping my mind on God. We used to sing in the old church, "*I woke up this morning with my mind stayed on Jesus.*" I must be intentional about whom I hang around and what I'm watching on TV. I must also be intentional about where I go, because I don't want to get distracted from that which God has for me.

Verse 34 says, "Wait for the Lord and keep His way." That word "keep" means "to hedge about; to guard, to watch over or to be circumspect." God wants us to guard, protect and be careful about doing what He wants us to do. I can't just do anything. I need to hear from God and make sure I'm in God's will—not only that I need to be watchful and not let what's going on around me to get into me.

Understand that people don't drown because they're standing in water. They don't drown because the water is up to their neck. They don't drown because they've been in water a long time. They drown because they allow too much water to get inside of them. In other words, they allow too much of that which is around them to get on the inside of them.

That's how we get in trouble. We let worry and anxiety get inside of us, therefore, preventing us from keeping God's way. Every now and then, you need to say to yourself, "No, these bills are not going to drown me; my supervisor is not going to drown me nor will my family, with all their drama, going to drown me! I might be in it, but I'm not going to let it get inside of me!"

"Wait for the Lord and keep His way, and He will exalt you to inherit the land." In this season, if I just make sure to stay focused on the Lord, the Bible says that God will exalt me. I won't have to market myself. I won't have to tell people I'm gifted. I won't have to try to get ahead. No, the Lord will exalt me!

It's funny, because I hear people say, "I'm grindin,'" "I'm on my grind" or "I'm getting my grind on." *Hey man, how's work? (I'm grinding everyday). How's school sister? (I'm on my grind). Hey, how's your family? (Man, we just grindin').* Let me put a Carron comma right here. You and I were not created to grind. You are not an ox, you are not a mule, neither are you a beast of burden. No, we weren't created to grind; we were created to be guided. Somebody ought to write that down. You weren't created to grind, but to be guided.

Don't confuse Old Testament *Theology* with New Testament *Christology.* Yes, in **Genesis 3:23,** God sent Adam to "till the ground" or to grind as a result of him listening to Eve and eating the fruit. But guess what? We are not Old Testament Christians. <u>We are on the other side of the cross</u>. Our faith was **reconstituted** and **reconstructed** when the Angel rolled the stone away, and we could look in and see that our Savior lives.

That's why Paul said in **Galatians 5:18,** *"But if you are led by the Spirit, you are not under the law."* Ok, y'all not feelin' Paul? Well, Jesus said in **John 13:16,** *"When the Spirit of truth comes, he will guide you into all the truth, for he will not speak on his own authority, but whatever he hears he will speak, and he will declare to you the things that are to come."* We are called to be guided, not grinding. We have the Holy Spirit living inside of us. That great church song says: *"Order my steps in your word, dear Lord; <u>lead me, guide me,</u> every day. Send your anointing Father I pray, order my steps in your word!"*

Wait for the Lord and keep His way, and He will exalt you to inherit the land. The Lord will not just exalt me, but God will exalt me to inherit the land. That which once belonged to the wicked will be ours. You might want to hold on to your seat, because God is about to shift some stuff. He's about to move some decimals in your bank account.

He's about to put you on the right person's mind. He's about to perform what you've been praying for. Not only that, but He's about to give to you that which should have been yours.

Remember, God promised the land to the Jews. So, they knew the land was their inheritance. How many of you know that in order to get your inheritance, there must be a death? In this season, debt is going to die, stress is going to die and unhealthy habits are going to die, unhealthy relationships are going to die! God will exalt you to inherit the land. Tell your neighbor, *"Get ready, get ready, get ready—it's on the way!"*

Not only will I inherit the land, but the text says, *"You will look on when the wicked are cut off."* I'm going to have a front row seat when the Lord cuts off the wicked. David said in **Psalm 23,** *"Thou prepares a table before me in the presence of my enemies."* That's how you know God is preparing your table, because your enemies keep getting closer. God can't do it until your enemies get close enough. They have to be close enough to pull up a chair and sit down! You need to go home and count your enemies. Then, tell the Lord, *"I'm going to need a table for 3, a table for 5, a table for 6."* Then say, *"Lord, tell them to bring their appetite!"*

Verse 35 sounds like it came straight from the cable news channels. *"I have seen a wicked, ruthless man, spreading himself like a green laurel tree."* That word, "ruthless," means "a powerful tyrant." "Spreading himself" literally means "to make himself naked" or "to uncover. "Green" means "to be prosperous or flourishing," while a laurel tree references a tree springing up or spontaneous growth.

Let's look at this again. Have you seen a wicked tyrant who has uncovered or exposed himself, look like he's prosperous and quickly spread his wickedness and ruthlessness all over the land?

I was thinking about this the other day. I paid a lot of money for my legal education, while y'all are getting a law degree for free. All you have to do is turn on the news and they're teaching you about grand juries and indictments; co-conspirators and immunity—campaign finance law. I'm thinking, *"You know how much money I had to pay to learn about the law? Now they're just giving it away!"*

Doesn't it feel like we are literally watching Verse 35 in real life, every day? How many more people need to be indicted? How many more people need to be convicted? How many more people need to be granted immunity? This really looks like a reality show, not The Apprentice but more like Survivor! We all looking to see who's not going to jail! Who'll be left on the island?

Let's look at **Verse 35-36 together,** *"I have seen a wicked, ruthless man, spreading himself like a green laurel tree. But he passed away, and behold, he was no more; though I sought him, he could not be found."* That's why I love the Bible. It tells you and me how God will deal with our enemies. Reading your Bible will help you get a good night's sleep. Reading your Bible will give you peace on your job. Reading your Bible will have you watching the exploits of this president with a bag of popcorn, just waiting to see how God is going to handle him. **Romans 15:4 says,** *"For whatever things were written before were written for our learning, that we through the patience and comfort of the Scriptures might have hope."*

God is reassuring us that our waiting and trusting in Him will not be in vain. Though the exploits of the wicked make it difficult, it is our godly discipline together with trusting God's Word that will guarantee our deliverance and protection from God.

Your assignment this week is to observe someone godly – someone who's had to wait on the Lord and somebody who had to endure wicked and the ruthless folks and look to see how they handled it. **Verse 37 says, "Mark the blameless and behold the upright, for there is a future for the man of peace."** The word, "mark," means, "to watch, to observe, to literally watch as out of a sense of duty."

Pray, "Lord, give me an example so I can stay on track, so I can keep my mind. Lord, send me an example to know how to hold on, because your word says, *'The race isn't given to the swift, nor the battle to the strong, but to he or she who endures until the end.'"*

Lastly and then I'm done. **Verses 39-40 say,** *"The salvation of the righteous is from the Lord; he is their stronghold in the time of trouble. The Lord helps them and delivers them; he delivers them from the wicked and saves them, because they take refuge in him. The salvation of the righteous is from the Lord."* The word, "salvation," means "rescue, deliverance, help, and safety." Many of us live everyday watching the wicked win by way of their wicked schemes. We wonder why we have to struggle so much and it appears as if the wicked get to skate through. This weighs very hard on our faith, on our self-esteem, our self-worth; it messes with our minds and can alter our approach to life.

The Good News is that my help, my rescue, my deliverance comes from the Lord. He is my stronghold in time of trouble, He's a rock in a weary land and He's my shelter in the times of a storm!

Verse 40 says, "*The Lord helps them and delivers them.*" The word "Lord," is translated ***Jehovah.*** Jehovah is the national name of God. It is the divine name God chose as His personal name by which He related specifically to His chosen or covenant people. In other words, God uses that name to show that He has a relationship with His people.

Sometimes we forget that we have a personal God. God is not some CEO you only see on Easter and Christmas (hint, hint). But no, we have a connection to God and not just a connection, but we are in covenant with God.

The Lord helps them and delivers them. The word, "help." means, "to surround, protect or aid." God is personally connected to us and is there to aid us. ***And delivers them.*** Deliver means to slip out, escape or cause to deliver. God is not just your personal protector, but He helps us to escape from the plans of the wicked.

I need somebody to know today that if you hold on, God will help you. If you hold on, God will deliver you. If you hold on, God can help you slip-out of some tight situations.

Let me illustrate it like this: About 30 years ago, a commuter flight was flying from Portland, Maine to Boston. The pilot, Henry Dempsey, heard an unusual noise in the rear of the plane. So, he turns over control to the co-pilot to go check it out.

He gets back to the tail of the plane and realizes the source of the noise. The rear door had not been properly latched prior to takeoff. Suddenly, the plane hits some turbulence, throwing Dempsey into the door and it flew open. Dempsey was instantly sucked out of the jet.

The co-pilot, seeing the red light that indicated an open door, immediately radios the nearest airport to tell them to prepare for an emergency landing. He tells them to send a helicopter to search the ocean, because the pilot had fallen out of the plane.

After the plane landed, they found Henry Dempsey holding on to the outdoor ladder of the plane with only his left foot still in the plane. Somehow, he caught the ladder, held on for 10 minutes, as the plane flew at nearly 200 mph and at 5000 feet. Then at landing, his head was only a foot off of the ground. It took airport personnel several minutes to pry his fingers from the ladder. The news in Maine did a story on him last year where they called him, "Hang on Hank."

That's all I came to tell you today, that you'll hit some turbulence in life and life is going to toss you around. But if you can just hold on, God will get you where you need to go.

- You might not get there how you thought you were going to get there, but God will get you there.
- Sometimes you'll want to let go, but hang on; God will get you there.
- The landing might be a little rough, but if you hold on, God will get you there!

Do I have some Hang on Hank's in the house?

- Hang on until God opens that door
- Hang on until God makes your enemies your footstool
- Hang on until God brings your family back together
- Hang on until we can end mass incarceration
- Hang on until we can cleanse the Whitehouse
- Hang on until no child or family goes to bed hungry
- Hold on until justice rolls down like waters and righteousness like a mighty stream

Rev. James Cleveland says it much better than me:

My way may not be easy
You did not say that it would be
But when it gets dark
I can't see my way
You told me to put my trust in Thee
That's why I'm asking you

Lord help me to hold out—I believe I can hold out—Lord help me to hold out;

Until, until, until my change comes!

CLOSING PRAYER

Dear God, help me to be patient while you are working. Remind me that your silence doesn't mean you are still and that while it feels like you are absent, the fact is, you are always active. I believe a change will come to my situation. I pray for patience and peace during the process. In Jesus' name I pray, Amen.

CHAPTER 8 - REFLECTION QUESTIONS

1. What are common distractions that make it difficult for us to wait on God?
2. How should our perspective change, realizing that God is my deliverer?
3. Why is it important to put on "blinders" while waiting on God?

CHAPTER 9

"Show Them Who You Are"

We are called to unapologetically let the light of Christ shine in
our lives. It is our light that God will use to change the world.

Matthew 5:13-16

The movie Black Panther has literally taken the world by storm. It
has grossed over a billion dollars worldwide, becoming the highest
grossing superhero film of all time and has really become more of a
movement than a **movie**. I hope you've seen the movie by now. If not,
this isn't much of a spoiler, but there is a scene in the movie where all the
tribes of Wakanda come together to decide who the next king will be.
Now understand, T'Challa's father, the previous king has died, so now
each tribe gets the chance to send out its best warrior to fight T'Challa
to see if he can wear the crown as king. They are all gathered at this
river and T'Challa (played by the brilliant Chadwick Boseman) begins
fighting one of the warriors from another tribe and looks like he's about
to lose. He's getting beaten left and right and being tossed around left
and right. All the while, his sister and mother can barely stand to watch
the beating that T'Challa is taking. Then, T'Challa's mother played by
the ageless, beautiful, bad and bodacious sister by the name of Angela
Bassett, yells out to her son in desperation, *"Show them who you are!"* It
is at that point that T'Challa reaches down deep and finds some extra
strength to fight and goes on to win the battle.

Every now and then, you and I find ourselves in situations where we have to show them who we are. When your coworker tries to show out on the job, you have to show them who you are. When your child or your grandchild want to walk around your house refusing to neither cook, clean nor contribute, you have to show them who you are. When church folk think that just because you're saved that they can say whatever they want to you, however they want to say it, you have to show them who you are!

In today's text, Jesus is preaching what we famously know to be the Sermon on the Mount. Christ is reaffirming to His followers their mandate and mission in the movement Jesus has started.

Let me give you the context to help you better appreciate the content.

Jesus, here in Matthew 5, is giving what we know to be the Sermon on the Mount. This sermon is what you may call, "The Manifesto of the Movement." It is Jesus laying out to His followers, in a succinct way, who they are, how they are to live and what they can expect to happen in the future.

Scholars describe this scene as the Moses motif. Much like Moses in Exodus when he comes down from Mt. Sinai, after having spent time with Lord, with the 10 Commandments, Jesus now in similar fashion is on a mountain and He is giving the people instructions from God. Jesus is now supplanting, succeeding and superseding Moses as the one who brings forth the instructions of God directly from the mouth of God. Jesus is ushering in a new world order. You may ask, "How so preacher?"

The 10 commandments were the law. They focused on what you should not do. Thou shalt not do this and that. Here, Jesus is focusing on what you must do. But most importantly, it's rooted in love.

Remember, Jesus is speaking to a group of people who are living on the margins of life. They are oppressed Galileans whose homeland is being both occupied and colonized by the Roman Empire. The Romans have come in and displaced the Galileans religiously, economically, governmentally, culturally, and in some instances, physically. This is what made Jesus such a huge problem, because He empowered and educated people that the world had written off; He encouraged and enlightened people the world didn't want anything to do with and elevated and emancipated people whom society did not value.

Isn't that what Jesus is still doing today? Is there anybody here who ever thought you'd be sitting in church on a Sunday morning? Is there anybody who ever thought that Jesus would use you in ministry (with all your stuff, with all of your mess)? Did you ever think God would use you to sing His praises, ordain you as a deacon or have you in administration? God literally picked some of us up, turned us around and placed our feet on solid ground! *When I think of the goodness of Jesus and all He has done for me, my soul cries Hallelujah, thank you Lord for saving me!*

Interestingly, Jesus begins this discourse by calling the people "blessed." *Blessed are the poor in spirit, blessed are the meek, blessed are those who hunger and thirst for righteousness.* That word, "*blessed,*" in Greek is translated "fortunate, well-off or privileged." Jesus, in just one word, has placed the people in a different social class, forcing them to reevaluate how they see themselves in light of how society has told them to see themselves.

Jesus is letting them know that society does not have the final say as to how you should view yourself. Is there anybody here, who on a Sunday morning, realize that I'm not what my paycheck says I am? I'm not what my ex says I am, neither what they say about me at work, nor am I the mistakes of my past. I am who God says I am! I know everyone is excited about the Royal family and the wedding of Meghan and Harry. I wish the sister all the success in the world, but they aren't the only royalty walking around here. **1 Peter 2:9, *"But you are a chosen generation, a royal priesthood, a holy nation, His own special people, that you may proclaim the praises of Him who called you out of darkness into His marvelous light;"*** I am who God says I am!

Then Jesus moves on and says even though you're blessed and well-off and privileged (v. 10-12) you'll still face persecution, but don't worry about it because great is your reward in heaven.

Look at verse 11, *"Blessed are you when others revile you and persecute you and utter all kinds of evil against you falsely on my account."* How many of you know that you'll face persecution in this life? For example, these days you can't even sit in a Starbucks to meet and conduct a business deal before they call the police on you just because of the color of your skin. As Ice Cube said, when you live in a society where "your skin is a sin," you're going to face persecution. When you just want to have a barbecue in the park and a woman with the "majority" skin tone feels it's her duty to call the police on you and then tries to turn the situation around and call herself a victim, you know you're dealing with persecution. Ok you not feeling them? I think about NBA player Sterling Brown of the Milwaukee Bucks, coming out of a Walgreens at two o'clock in the morning, walking to his own car and getting harassed and beaten and tased over what should have been a parking ticket, you better believe you're going to face some persecution!

Right after Jesus speaks of them facing persecution, He says, ***"You are the salt of the earth."*** Salt had different meanings in Matthew's day. It meant sacrifice, loyalty and covenant fidelity, purification and seasoning. In fact, salt was so valuable that the Romans sometimes paid their soldiers with it. If a soldier did not carry out his duties, others would say, "He is not worthy of his salt." That's where we get the expression, "Worth his salt." Jesus is focusing more on the seasoning and preservative uses for salt.

Jesus says, "You" (for emphasis). What Jesus is saying is "You—the people here, not the Pharisees—are the salt of the earth. Now, the Pharisees are standing there as Jesus was declaring this. Jesus has literally demoted the Pharisees in front of the people that they were oppressing. Jesus says, "Don't worry about the side-eye they're giving—remember, you pay them, they make money off of your labor and other forms of exploitation they invoke" (I'm paraphrasing).

You are the salt of the earth! That is why nonviolent protest and boycotts are important, whether it's people protesting the government, a corporation or any form of racial injustice. When ordinary people come together, what they're really saying is we are the salt, not you. Yes, we may have low paying jobs and not have high social status, but we're the ones that got you elected, pay your salary and buy your products. We are the seasoning that gives your life flavor; we are the preservative that allows you to continue in business. We are the salt of the earth!

But if salt loses its flavor, it is no longer good for anything. In Palestine, flakes of salt form on the rock shores of the Dead Sea at night.

In the morning, the sun rises. Under its heat, the salt loses its saltiness and blends with the shore and loses its distinctiveness.

Jesus is telling them that you must always be who God called you to be regardless of the situation or circumstance. Don't try to blend in when you were created to stand out. The world needs your flavor, your gifts, your anointing, your calling—you are the salt of the earth.

Not only that, but Jesus goes on to tells them, *"You are the light of the world."* The word, "light." Here in Greek means "to shine or to make manifest." The primary function of light is not to be seen, but to let other things be seen as they are. Light doesn't exist for its own benefit. I don't turn on the light in a dark room to see the light. I turn it on to see the room and what's in it.

When people see me, I ought to be shining a light on the God that is in me. Help me out Mary Mary, *"You think I'm so fresh, you think I'm so clean, you think I'm so sweet, it's the God in me..."*

Then Jesus says, *"A city set on a hill cannot be hidden."* He is speaking to the communal nature of letting our lights shine. When we all get together, it's like a city on a hill, unavoidable and seen by everyone. He describes the faith community as a city. In other words, we should be working together in a way that shines light on God's original intent for man. We should be showing the world how to do business, how to care for the sick and vulnerable, how to raise our children and how to administer justice and demonstrate God's love for all people. The world should be able to look to the church, and we should be so full of light that we look like a city on a hill that you can't take your eyes off of.

The important thing about both salt and light is that both of them can't do it on their own. Salt doesn't make itself salty and a light must be lit in order for it to shine.

These metaphors that Jesus uses clearly identify God as the source. God gives us light not just for ourselves, to draw attention to ourselves, but so that people would see our good works and glorify God in heaven. We are called to unapologetically let the light of Christ shine in our lives. It is our light that God will use to change the world.

Lastly, Jesus says in **Matthew 5:16**, *"Let your light so shine before men, that they may see your good works and glorify your Father in heaven."* Jesus says to let your light shine. Notice this isn't a suggestion.

We are commanded to let our light shine, not privately, but publicly. The light of Christ is to shine in and through us "before men." In other words, this is a public exhibition of light. It is important to notice that the "light" is not equal with good works. Rather, the light illuminates the good works in such a way that people notice them and glorify God. What is it that lights up our works to the glory of God? I believe it is our verbal testimony to Jesus Christ. Good works by themselves are not light; they must be illuminated by words that direct attention and tribute to the Lord Jesus Christ.

When you give somebody some money, tell him or her, "God bless you." When you buy them some groceries, tell them. "The Lord put it on my heart." When you give them a ride to work, tell them, "I'm just glad to be used by God. I'm trying to shine the light on my good works, not to make me look good, but that they may glorify my Father in Heaven."

The next time they congratulate you at work on your promotion, tell them, "Yes, I worked hard. Yes, I made some sacrifices. Yes, I made some good decisions, *but if it had not been for the Lord on my side I wouldn't be here today.*" The next time God heals your body, make sure you tell folks, "Yes, I started eating, right. Yes, I started exercising. Yes, I took all of my medication, but there is still a balm in Gilead who heals the sin sick soul."

I wrote this book to encourage you to show them who you are:

Show them—I might not be what I want to be, but thank God I'm not what I used to be.
Show them—I might be down but I'm not out.
Show them—that Greater is He that is in me than he who is in the world
Show them—I'm more than a conqueror
Show them—that there is no weapon formed against me that will prosper.
Show them—until justice rolls down like water and righteousness like a mighty stream
Show them—that where I am right now is not where I'll always be.

Can we go back to Sunday School? *This little light of mine. I'm gonna let it shine...Jesus gave it to me, I'm going to let it shine...all in my home,*

*I'm going to let it shine...everywhere I go, let it shine, let it shine, let it shine...***Show them who you are, show them who you are, show them who you are!**

CLOSING PRAYER

Dear God, thank you for giving me a light to shine. I know the world, on a daily basis, wants me to conform or change in some way how you created me to be. Give me the confidence and dexterity to never be afraid or back down from who I am and what I was created to do. In Jesus' name, I pray, Amen.

CHAPTER 9 - REFLECTION QUESTIONS

1. Why did Jesus declare that we are the light of the world?
2. Why is it important to "show them who you are?"
3. What affect do we have on others when we openly embrace who God created us to be?

CHAPTER 10

"No Weapon"

As we remember the 50th Anniversary of the assassination of
Rev. Dr. Martin Luther King Jr., his life and legacy coupled with
his words and works help to inspire and instruct us today as we
activate our faith on behalf of our church and community.
God has promised to protect us. We will live to complete
our calling, because we are His chosen people.

Isaiah 54:17

This year, we celebrate the 50th anniversary of the assassination of
Dr. King on April 4th, 1968. There have been tributes this past year
including a big one that took place down in Memphis around the time
of his death in April. However, today we will examine and look to draw
from his life and legacy, along with his words and works, and connect
them to how relevant they are today to what God is calling us to do.

First, I want to look at something in Dr. King's life that occurred 60
years ago. On September 20, 1958, Dr. King was doing a book signing
for his first book, *Stride Toward Freedom—The Montgomery Story*, at
Blumstein's Department Store on 125th street in Harlem, New York.

While signing books, a woman by the name of Izola Ware Curry
walked up and asked him "Are you Dr. King?" Unknown to Dr. King,
underneath her nice outfit was a letter opener and a .25 caliber pistol.
Ms. Curry walked up to Dr. King, draws the letter opener from her purse
and stabs him in the chest. Dr. King could not immediately remove the

blade; it was too close to his heart. He was told not to move an inch, not to speak. He was rushed to Harlem Hospital for emergency surgery. The doctors later told him that any sudden movement — so much as a sneeze — could have cost him his life.

Dr. King recalled this near tragedy during his final sermon, "I've Been to the Mountain Top," which was preached the evening before his death. He talked about being in the hospital after the surgery and receiving letters from everyone, including high-ranking government officials to everyday people. In that sermon, Dr. King spoke of a letter he received from a White girl in nineth grade from White Plains, NY. She wrote about reading in the paper that had Dr. King sneezed he would have died. She told Dr. King in her letter that she was happy he did not sneeze.

> Then Dr. King before recounting all of the civil rights victories that would follow that fateful day went on to say: *"I want to say tonight that I, too, am happy that I didn't sneeze."*

Dr. King, here, is recalling the fact that he literally came to within inches of losing his life. But he survived. It was a close call, but he survived. It should have killed him, but he survived.

I just got a question for the people of God today. Has the devil ever come close to taking you out? Is there a time where you can look over your life and know you should have died and been buried in your grave? I'm talking about the high-risk surgery you came out of or the car accident you walked away from. Maybe it was you being delivered from an abusive relationship or from the stress on your job that had you taking all types of medication.

Every now and then, you need to lift up holy hands and give God praise that you're still here! I don't have all the money I want, but I'm still here. I might be on medication every day, but I'm still here. I walk a little slower than I used to, but I'm still here. I got myself in some tight situations, but I'm still here. I had some friends turn on me, but I'm still here!

Kurt Carr put it this way:

I almost let go, I felt like I couldn't take life anymore, my problems had me boud, depression weighed me down. But God held me close, so I wouldn't let go, God's mercy kept me, so I wouldn't let go.

In today's text, we see God reminding His people about His promises of restoration and salvation to them. He let's them know that what they went through before, they won't go through again. He is saying to us that we survived, but things are about to get sweeter; we lived through tragedy, but He's about to set us on a new trajectory.

Let me give you the context to help you better appreciate the content.

The prophet Isaiah's name means, "Yahweh is Salvation" or "Salvation is of the Lord." The book of Isaiah reads like a miniature Bible. The first 39 chapters (much like the Old Testament's first 39 books of the Bible) talk about judgment upon immoral and idolatrous men and women. They portray humankind's need for a Savior. While the last 27 chapters (much like the New Testament with 27 books) declare a message of hope. Also, it declares that God will provide salvation. God is the Sovereign One and Israel's Savior.

Chapter 54 speaks about the people having returned to God and that He will bless them and restore them. The image is that of God, the faithful husband, forgiving Israel, the unfaithful wife, and restoring her to the place of blessing. The nation was "married" (so to speak) at Mt. Sinai, but she committed adultery by turning to other gods. Because of this, and her moral depravity, political corruption and social injustice, the Lord had to abandon her temporarily. However, the prophets promise that Israel will be restored when the Messiah comes and establishes His new Kingdom.

God tells them not to fear and that just as He made a covenant with Noah that the waters would not flood the earth again, God will no longer be angry with them nor rebuke them now that they are in a covenant of peace. In addition to that covenant of peace, God will protect them from any attacks of outside enemies.

Verse 17 says, *"No weapon that is fashioned against you shall succeed, and you shall refute every tongue that rises against you in judgment. This is the heritage of the servants of the Lord and their vindication from me, declares the Lord."*

No weapon—that word, "weapon," in Hebrew is translated as "something prepared; any apparatus, a weapon." How many of you know that the devil has something prepared for the people of God? Not only that, the text goes on to say that *No weapon that is fashioned (or formed) against you shall succeed.* The word "formed (or fashioned)" in Hebrew literally means "squeezing into shape or to mold into a form like a potter."

In other words, whatever weapon has been prepared and made specifically with you in mind to attack you, right where you are vulnerable, will not succeed.

How many of you know that the devil knows exactly where to attack you? He knows your weaknesses. He knows what you like. He knows what gets on your nerves. He knows what areas you are weak in faith. He knows what to bring up from your past to make you doubt yourself. He knows what to use in your present to frustrate you. He knows what it is about your future that causes you to have anxiety and worry.

But this Bible that we believe, this Chapter that we've chosen, this Verse that we are viewing says, *"No Weapon (not some weapons, not a few weapons, not even 1 weapon) formed or fashioned against you shall prosper or succeed!"*

Notice the text doesn't say it won't be formed. Don't think because God promised to protect you that the enemy's not plotting. Just because you're saved doesn't mean the devil won't take his best shot. Just because you know Christ doesn't mean that your enemies are not conspiring against you right now. All of these things will happen, but God said it won't work; the enemy won't win and his scheme will be spoiled.

That's why, every now and then, you need to remind yourself of who you are. Remind yourself that imbedded in your bloodline, directly deposited into your DNA, fixed within the framework of your family tree, is a long line of folks who look like you and me, who have had every weapon thrown against them.

As Black people in America, we must think of how many weapons have been formed against us:

- **Slavery**— For 246 years, our foremothers and forefathers were whipped and beaten; raped and stripped of their humanity and even had their children taken from them and sold.
- **Shortly after the civil war, Black Codes** were put in place to restrict the movement of Blacks, thereby, forcing them to work for Whites in a labor economy based on low wages and death.
- **Then Convict Leasing**— This is where if you're convicted of vagrancy, blacks could be imprisoned, and they also received sentences for a variety of petty offenses. States began to lease convict labor to the plantations and other facilities seeking labor, as the freedmen were trying to withdraw and work for themselves. This provided prisoner labor to private parties, such as plantation owners and corporations. It also provided the states with a new source of revenue during years when they were financially strapped, and lessees profited by the use of forced labor at below market rates.
- **We all know about Jim Crow, which existed for nearly 100 years,** where State and local laws were used to enforce racial segregation. Using the language of "separate but equal," but the public facilities, transportation and schools for Blacks were always inferior to those used by Whites. It was simply another system used to restrict the civil liberties and civil rights of Blacks.
- **KKK (Klu Klux Klan)**—a White terrorist organization consumed with a hatred toward Blacks and other minorities, who often used violence and murder (including lynching) to suppress African-Americans from achieving full citizenship.
- **I also thought about the Tuskegee Experiment**—a malicious, unethical, and reprehensible study done by the U.S. Public Health Service between 1932-1972. Black men in Alabama were unknowingly injected with Syphilis and medical professionals watched them die in order to better understand the disease and determine proper treatment doses.

- **Sterilizing Black women in this country—After WWII, there was a eugenics movement formed.** There was a belief by the majority in the disposability of certain women and that they should be sterilized, because they fell into certain categories like being poor, mentally ill, or minorities. **In some instances, they fit all three categories. In North Carolina alone, some 7,600 people were sterilized.** Eighty-five percent of those sterilized were women and girls, while 40 percent were minorities (most of whom were black). This was part of a eugenics plan under the belief that measures should be taken to prevent "undesirables" from reproducing so that problems such as poverty and substance abuse would be eliminated in future generations. Most of these sterilizations were not done with the patients' permission.
- **Crack sent into our neighborhoods.** We know for a fact that during the early 1980's and early 1990's, the U.S. Government deliberately flooded our communities with crack cocaine. This resulted in the destroying of Black families and communities and the so-called War on Drugs, which sent many of our Black men to jail.

Pastor, why are you reminding us about all of the attacks against Black people? I need to remind you that every weapon that has been formed against us has not worked. That's why they hate us! They hate us because everything they have tried has not worked. Every attempt to assassinate us as a people has been aborted. Every time America has tried to eliminate us, God has elevated us higher. Every attempt at group governmental homicide has led to God proving to be a very present help in time of trouble.

We have come over a way that with tears has been watered,
We have come, treading our path through the blood of the slaughtered,
Out from the gloomy past,
Till now we stand at last
Where the white gleam of our bright star is cast.

Allow me for a moment to place a Carron comma in this sermon. This past week as I watched the marathon known by most as the funeral of the late, great, brilliant singer, performer and civil rights activist known simply as Aretha, there were some words that came from the pulpit that I think need to be addressed.

Now understand I'm not in the business of going after other preachers; that's God's job. But when I hear things being broadcast on the world's stage about Black people that I know not to be true I have to say something.

When I heard talk about a Black woman being unable to raise a Black man at the funeral of a Black woman who happened to raise 4 Black men by herself, that is a problem. Would it be better to have a father there? Of course, but don't tell me it can't be done.

When I hear terms like Black-on-Black crime, I cringe, because there is no such thing. Crime is crime. If you study any statistics, you'll see that most crimes are based upon relationship, proximity, and opportunity. Thus, Black folks kill more Black folks because we're in proximity of each other, just like White folks kill more White folks because of proximity and relationship and opportunity. You never hear White-on-White crime, but they say Black on Black crime as a way of saying that there is some type of underlying moral deficiency or criminal chromosome imbedded in the DNA of Black people. I just can't accept that. We as a people cannot accept that.

Don't tell me that Black Lives only matter when a police officer kills an African-American and not when one of our own kills another, because our church has gone out on prayer walks after shootings in this community to show that killing is unacceptable in any shape, form or fashion. To this day we continue to work in the community to curb the violence.

Don't talk to me about Black fathers not being in the home, when this country has done everything it could do to destroy the Black family. The Mexican border is not the first time this country has separated minorities from their families. When 1-in-3 Black men are expected to go into the criminal justice system, when unemployment and underemployment plague our communities, when Black men are being shot and killed by police and White vigilantes all of the time, it's hard to talk about a lack of Black fathers in the home! This corrupt system is locking them up and killing them in record numbers.

The time is out to blame the victim. The time is up for respectability politics and conservative talking points. Yes, we, just like every other race, have internal issues, but let's not act like a lot of our internal issues aren't the result of external (American) influence.

People of God, there is greatness inside of you. God has kept us over and through many toils and snares; dangers seen and unseen—and despite every attack that has come against us, we're still here. That's why you can't give up, because God has shown us through the years that no weapon formed against us shall prosper. If our ancestors didn't give up on slave ships or through segregation, through being called boy and girl or aunt Nellie as an adult; if they didn't give up, when having to use outhouses and not having a chance to graduate from school, then how can we talk about giving up when we have homes, degrees, 401 K's, cell phones, the internet and social media? Could you imagine what our ancestors could have done with all that we have today?

My sisters and brothers, God has promised to protect us. We will live to complete our calling, because we are His chosen people. I like the next part of **Verse 54:** *"and you shall refute every tongue that rises against you in judgment."* **The New King James Version states it this way,** *"And every tongue which rises against you in judgment You shall condemn."* In other words, folks who try to talk about you, gossip about you or try to sabotage your career or relationship, every verbal attack shall be condemned. Don't worry about what folks have to say about you. God is giving you and me the power to negate and counter whoever believes they can talk about the elect of God.

This week, I want you to write down every attack coming against you. I want you to look at that list every morning and after you've read this list, I want you to recite this verse. I want you to put the Word to work and then work the Word! God said in **Jeremiah 1:12** that *"He is watching over His Word in order to perform it."* God will do what he said he would do.

The last part of **Verse 17,** *"This is the heritage of the servants of the Lord and their vindication from me, declares the Lord."* This is your heritage, your birthright, to have the protection of God over your life. Just imagine what your life would be like if you really believed that the enemy wouldn't win and that he can't win. Just imagine how our lives would be if you and I really believed and acted as if we are really surrounded by the protection of Almighty God.

Not only that, but if you really believed that when it's all said and done, God will vindicate you. God will defend you. God will uphold you. God will exonerate you. God will clear your name.

God wants us to see the future like it's right now. He wants your backbone to straighten up. He wants you to watch and pray, be concerned but not worried, strategize but don't be scared; be alert but not alarmed. You will not die before completing your assignment.

- **Dr. King was stabbed, but he didn't die, because his purpose was not complete**
- **Nelson Mandela spent 27 years in prison, essentially as a political prisoner, but he didn't die, because his purpose was not complete**
- **They put Daniel in the lions' den, but he didn't die, because his purpose was not complete**
- **Shadrach, Meshach and Abednego, were thrown in to the fiery furnace for not worshiping the king's idol, but they didn't die, because their purpose was not complete**
- **The apostle Paul was whipped, bitten by a snake, and shipwrecked, but he didn't die, because his purpose was not complete.**

Is there anybody here who says, "Pastor, I should be on that list?"

- I was sick in my body, but I didn't die, because my purpose was not complete
- I walked away from a car accident, but I didn't die, because my purpose was not complete
- I survived a heart attack, but I didn't die, because my purpose was not complete
- I endured foreclosure, but I didn't die, because my purpose was not complete

- My marriage ended, but I didn't die, because my purpose was not complete
- My close friend walked out on me, but I didn't die, because my purpose was not complete

Our faith has enabled us to <u>endure</u> and be <u>empowered</u> at the same time. Every attack against our advancement has eventually collapsed when coming against our strength and steadfastness. Keep believing, keep trusting, and keep marching on until victory is won.

Fred Hammond was right when sang:

No weapon formed against me shall prosper, it won't work...There just ain't one, There just ain't one weapon...

CLOSING PRAYER

Dear God, you know all of our trials and tribulations. You know what we go through on a daily basis. It is because you know and care that I can be at peace—knowing that everything is going to be alright. Help me to stay reminded that, though attacks will come, at the end of the day, no weapon formed against me shall prosper. In Jesus' name I pray, Amen.

CHAPTER 10 - REFLECTION QUESTIONS

1. Why is it reassuring to know that no weapon or attack or circumstance will succeed against us?
2. When going through the challenges of life, why is it important to know and understand your history?
3. Moving forward, how do you see this chapter changing your perspective about your problems?

Printed in the United States
By Bookmasters